# ADVENTURESS

# ADVENTURESS

## *Women Exploring the Wild*

CAROLINA AMELL

**PRESTEL**

Munich · London · New York

# KRISTIN ADDIS
# THE SOLO TRAVELER

*I've learned more about myself by traveling and adventuring alone than I ever could have any other way.*

I never feel more empowered than when I'm out on my own. Whether it's making it to the mountain summit just in time for sunrise after hiking solo in the dark, getting picked up by a friendly driver while hitchhiking abroad, or getting invited to do something unique with locals because there's room for just one more, I've learned more about myself by traveling and adventuring alone than I ever could have any other way.

I grew up in a suburb of Los Angeles. I didn't spend a lot of time deep in the mountains, lost in a forest, or staring up at a sky full of stars. I did not start off wanting to do this, or having the confidence to do so many things alone that other people are scared to do. I grew into this person little by little with each passing year of traveling solo around the world.

It started with a career in mergers and acquisitions in my early twenties. I was doing quite well for someone my age, both professionally and financially, but I was miserable. All my life I had done what I thought I was supposed to do. I got good grades and honors in school, worked hard at all my part-time jobs, and built an impressive resume, because I thought it would make me happy – except it didn't.

Ten years ago, I closed one of the biggest deals my firm had ever touched and watched as they congratulated my male superior, who did 1 percent of the work, if that, instead of me, who did 99 percent. I agonized over it for months, but after four years I finally decided to quit that job and buy a one-way ticket to Bangkok to see if freedom felt better than money. I didn't know if my dream of becoming a travel writer would come true, but one thing I knew for sure—I wasn't going back. I wasn't going to watch someone else get credit for what I did ever again, no matter what it took.

I had a small amount of savings that I started my journey with. I stayed in nothing but shared dorms, taking local transportation for pennies on the dollar, and eating only street food for a few years. I hitchhiked when I started to run out of money, hoping my blog might one day make enough money to sustain my travels so that I wouldn't have to go back to a cubicle.

I never thought I would be the person who liked strapping 55 pounds to my back and hiking through the wilderness without showering for days on end. I never saw myself standing on the side of the road in China with my thumb up hitching a ride. Over the last 10 years, I traveled solo through Southeast Asia, signing up for 10-day silent meditation retreats in Thailand, painting murals in exchange for free nights in hostels in Laos, eating delicious street food, and meeting amazing people to whom I still am close to this day. I have hitchhiked through two provinces of China, moved to Berlin, Germany, on an artist visa for over four years, spent a cumulative eight months on the African continent, and done several multi-day backpacking adventures by myself. Sometimes I look back on the girl in her early twenties who thought that her dreams should all revolve around climbing a corporate ladder and wonder what she would

*right* **Golden hour on Rialto Beach, Washington State.**

*previous page* **Goodbye Earth, hello Mars. The first time I came to Utah, I had no plan at all. I just took a rental camper and went. It was back then that I realized dispersed camping and public lands were a thing and that you could just keep going forever and never run out of things to see and places to go, like the Bentonite Hills in this photo.**

Sometimes I look back on the girl in her early twenties and wonder what she would have thought if she knew how things would end up—that she became someone who she never thought she would be.

have thought if she knew how things would end up—that she became someone who she never thought she would be.

I never thought I would be my own boss, writing a travel blog that is now read by millions of people each year. Each time it began by saying yes to something small, which then turned into something bigger, and it led me to adventures all across the world, covering over 60 countries that I visited on my own over the past decade.

That's not to say it was always sunshine and roses. There were bleak moments when it seemed like I'd have to quit it all, when my bank account teetered on the edge, and when I considered deciding that I'd had a good run, but it was over now. It took years of living on a dime, keeping the faith, taking writing jobs that paid the bills but ultimately underpaid me, and feeling like an imposter before I finally saw financial success.

*left* **A selfie I took in Wild Willy's Hot Spring, Mammoth Lakes, California. I was about four months pregnant here and had to be clever with angles.**

*top* **The Philippines, one of my favorite countries to travel solo in. Southeast Asia is where I kickstarted my solo journey, and subsequently, my blog.**

But every time I reached those eleventh-hour moments, something would work out. I got a freelance writing job I'd applied for that paid $600 per month, guaranteed for a year, and at the time, that was the confidence I needed to keep going. More opportunities followed, and eventually my little business grew. Besides, even though financial abundance and being recognized as a success is a nice part of being able to do this as my job, it was always about the freedom more than anything. One of the most important things I learned was that even though I wasn't the smartest person out there—and I wasn't the absolute best writer or photographer, although I was good—it didn't matter, because I had grit. I never wanted to give up.

I'm lucky that I met the love of my life at a campfire in Namibia and that we are starting a family. I know for sure that we will share our love of travel and adventures with our children, and I'll always feel glad that I took a leap of faith. I love the adventures that I get to have by myself, even though they're not so frequent these days, and that's totally fine with me. If the past 10 years have taught me anything, it's that it's never too late to take a leap of faith, and that there's almost always something better on the other side.

**Stargazing in Hawai'i, one of the most popular destinations on my site.**

*left* **Beautiful Iceland. I led women's tours around the world, including Iceland. One summer, 16 of us hiked through Landmannalaugar over the course of two weeks—an epic adventure.**

*top* **Swimming with sharks in New Mexico. Being an avid scuba diver and free diver has not only opened up the underwater world for me, but also opportunities to work with tour companies and tourism boards to promote diving trips.**

*right* **Having a blissful moment in the Philippines.**

*next page left* **Being in the water with humpback whales is a life-changing experience I cannot put into words. I've done it at least five times now, and it never gets old.** *right* **In the past 10 years, I have gone from a finance girl to a badass woman who runs the biggest solo female travel blog in the English-speaking world. With a new baby and family, I am curious, optimistic, and excited for the future, and strive to continue living life fearlessly and adventurously.**

# BELÉN CASTELLÓ
# THE BIKEPACKER

*Suddenly I felt I had the world at my feet, a blank canvas to cover with stories and experiences. I had no doubt I wanted to travel as far as I could.*

I am living a life now that I definitely would not have envisioned for myself as a kid. But would my young self be proud of the decisions I am making today? I think she definitely would.

I grew up in Valencia, Spain, and had the most pleasant and comfortable ordinary childhood one could wish for. When I was younger, my parents would take my brother and me to the mountains on vacation, and I loved spending time outdoors. But I have always been very diligent and hardworking, which meant that, when I turned 18, I couldn't think of any other reliable option but to go to university and study for a career that would fuse my technical and artistic interests. This was architecture.

I knew I wanted to travel and do "other stuff"—whatever that meant—but my perfectionism and, back then, inability to think outside the box I'd grown up in told me I first had to finish my studies and secure a future that was safe and stable. That's what everyone does, right? I skipped studying abroad to finish the six-year degree as fast as possible in order to get some experience in the field and start earning my first salary. I applied for jobs all around the world (finally, some travel!) and, just as I was preparing for an interview in Shanghai, I received an offer to work in Amsterdam. This is where Tristan, my partner, and I met.

A few months later I got offered another job in London by an office I had previously applied to. Hungry as I was for change and discovery, I decided to move there after six months of living in the Netherlands. London was a great experience and shaped me professionally, but as I got more comfortable with the lifestyle, the dream of traveling started knocking on the door again, becoming stronger every day. I hadn't given in to it before, because it had never felt like the right moment—not enough money, the risk of losing my spot at university, the uncertainty of finding a job—but these concerns faded as my relationship with Tristan grew stronger. He seduced me into giving traveling by bicycle a go, and I trusted him.

After nearly two years of office work, I decided that now was the right moment to take on this life-changing experience. Having taken the decision mentally, I then spent one more year slowly preparing myself for the transition. Even though I had a great job that gave me the chance to work on amazing architectural projects around the world, my days started feeling longer and longer. I'd look out of the window by my desk trying to understand why I was sitting there for more than eight hours a day facing a computer, while the sun cast warmth on the world outside, with all those many places waiting to be explored.

I had also never really cycled before, at least not seriously. Amsterdam had taught me the necessary skills to stay balanced on a bicycle, plus a fair bit of traffic tactics. London honed that skill, as I always cycled to and from work through the busy streets. I was ready for the challenge. I had the savings, a good CV for future use, no serious attachments, and the drive to try something very different. It was decided—we were going to discover the world by bicycle.

Suddenly I felt I had the world at my feet, a blank canvas to cover with stories and experiences. I had no doubt I wanted to travel as far as I could. My dreams were in Vietnam, Peru, Tajikistan, Canada, Namibia, longing for a grand escape. But

**Standing by the cliffside of Sierra Salvada in the Basque Country, Spain, in 2020, when international travel was out of question. It was the perfect opportunity to get to know my own "backyard."**

The funny thing is that, as naive as I am, I never really understood what bike travel actually entailed.

*left* **Pushing my way through the last section of the Pfitscher Joch pass right by the border between Italy and Austria. Hike-a-biking is tough but also fun when you are able to connect smooth gravel sections whilst enjoying stunning views.**

*top* **Taking a quick break by an empty beach in the island of Formentera, Spain. The Balearic Islands are packed with people for most of the year, so visiting in the low season—when there's barely anyone to be seen—made the experience very special.**

Tristan made a good point: Since I had never camped out or ridden a bike further than a few miles before, it made sense to stay closer to home in case things didn't work out.

We chose Norway to start with, a country that not only made sense seasonally (as we were starting in summer), but also felt wild yet safe, and offered an abundance of opportunities to stop for the night and camp out. This four-month trip would be my testing ground to decide whether bike travel was for me and whether our relationship would be able to survive the shift from long distance to being together 24 hours a day.

The funny thing is that, as naive as I am, I never really understood what bike travel actually entailed. On day one, I faced my first 12 percent climb. As heavily loaded as we were, my legs didn't have the strength to push me and my gear up the steep hill. I felt overwhelmed and it suddenly hit me: How was

## Day after day I felt my body and mind getting stronger.

I going to cross a mountainous country like Norway if I was already struggling (a lot) on the first climb? I had a small panic attack and couldn't breathe properly. I cried, sat down by the side of the road, and shared my fears with Tristan. Eventually, I found the strength to pull myself together and walk up the path with silent tears running down my face. I kept telling myself: This is still so much better than being at the office.

Day after day I felt my body and mind getting stronger. Suddenly, I no longer had to dismount on the climbs and could cover way more ground. I realized I loved being outdoors, pedaling through the ever-changing landscapes, taking it all in. Sometimes, I found myself complaining about the rain, the mosquitos, or my sore muscles, but the grumpiness went away just as fast as it came. By the top of the next pass, the next meal, or the next camping spot, the sensation of fulfillment and joy erased any traces of tough times with a monumental view, hot meal, or clear sky bursting with stars as a reward. Four months into the journey, I was sold. I wanted to keep riding my bike for years to come.

Bike travel must be one of the best ways (if not the best) to see the world, as it offers a sense of freedom and ease no other means seem to be able to match. I love how it makes me feel strong but vulnerable at the same time. And I enjoy the speed. It's enough to cover a good distance without missing the details, while being able to connect with the locals and surroundings. You get as far as your body will take you—and you'd be surprised how far that can be!

But how to make this lifestyle a lasting one? Even though my relationship with social media has, for years, felt like a rollercoaster of unhealthy sentiments, I am still extremely grateful for the opportunities Instagram has given me. My early interest in photography and fondness for documenting our journeys while sharing our adventures on this app meant that, very slowly, brands started to be interested in our lifestyle. Soon enough, our passion for bike travel and encouraging others to try out this life-changing experience (whether for a weekend escape

**Taking in the views during blue hour whilst setting up our home for the night on a beach in Menorca, Spain. The serenity of this evening was unreal, especially at night when the skies were covered with twinkling stars.**

*left* **Getting ready for bed. Our life on the road has a set routine and in the evenings, I'm in charge of making our tent cosy.**

*top* **Being out on the road for the whole day definitely works up your appetite! This evening, after having climbed to the foothills of the Picos de Europa in northern Spain, I couldn't stop checking in on dinner, hoping I'd be able to munch on it very soon.**

*right* **Why follow the roads when you can explore unmapped trails? It's so much more fun when you don't really know where a path will take you.**

It is true that in order to chase our flexible dreams we've had to sacrifice very important things.

or an open-end trip around the world) meant that our photo and video documentation also became our portfolio.

It is true that in order to chase our flexible dreams—living relatively detached from the traditional paths—we've had to sacrifice very important things: for example, not having the comfort of stability in our lives or certainty in our future. It's a high price to pay in the long run, as unconsciously, fear creeps through the backdoor of your mind in your weakest moments. But as compensation, I get to live a life that I love, control, and crave.

I've already cycled all round Europe, North America, and Central Asia. And as I get more experienced and comfortable in my skin, I know I'll be able to find a healthier balance between bike travel and my own, personal sense of "home." For now, the list of places I still want to discover on two wheels is long enough to keep me pedaling for many years to come.

So, here it comes: Go ride your bike. You might just be surprised by how much you'll love it.

*left* **Exploring the pastures of Velika Planina in Slovenia where, together with a spectacular landscape, you can find a picturesque herders' dwellings settlement.**

*right* **There are two of us in the team and since neither of us has a stand for our bikes, I've earned myself the title of "best human stand." No bike falls on the ground during my watch!**

*next page left* **I love starting my days rolling downhill. Corsica was full of dreamy winding roads and the mountainous backdrops often left me speechless.** *right* **One of the best things about taking quieter paths is discovering small towns and villages where locals are not so used to tourists passing by. Connecting with them is one of the best parts of bike travel.**

# GINA JOHANSEN
# THE EXPEDITIONIST

*My heart beats for Arctic expeditions, and I dream about Antarctica being my next project.*

I am a Swedish girl who has found her paradise in the Norwegian mountains. I spend most of my free time outdoors, both on shorter trips and on longer expeditions that take a couple of months. I hike, run, and ski in the mountains and I love both warm summer days and cold and frosty winter ones. However, my heart beats a little more for Arctic expeditions, and I dream about Antarctica being my next project. I wasn't born into the outdoor life, as many Norwegians and Swedes are, but that doesn't stop me filling my life with adventure.

I have never set any limits on my dreams and have always been determined to find a way to fulfill them. For me, it started with horses. As a child, I dreamed of traveling the world to work for the best stables. I spent all my free time around the horses at home, worked hard, and always wanted to learn something new. The hard work paid off and at age 15 I left school to work with horses full time. For 12 years I worked with both show jumping and racehorses around the world and lived my childhood dream. After I had worked in the horseracing industry in Australia for eight years, I was looking for new adventures in my life and got introduced to trail running. It didn't take long before I fell in love with the beauty of the mountains. I loved to push myself further and explore new places. My ideas and dreams just kept growing and I came up with the idea to cycle the east coast of Australia from Sydney to Cairns. This was my first serious trip—I did it together with my ex-boyfriend. I loved the adventure, the people we met along the way, and the new places to explore each day.

**A little stop to soak in the beautiful view on Besseggen in Jotunheimen national park on my 1,640-mile-long hike through Norway.**

After spending a bit of time in Cairns and New Zealand, I was back in Sydney working with horses. I had missed it, but it wasn't long until I was no longer satisfied with work. I couldn't get my mind off the mountains, and dreamed about new adventures. I wanted to travel to Europe and run in the mountains there. I worked and saved money to go over for three months to run races and explore the Alps, but few weeks before my trip I injured myself due to running. This was going to change my life. My body needed more time to get used to the impact of running, but I couldn't stop dreaming about another adventure in the mountains. I started to realize how little I had seen of the country I am from. I was born and grew up in Sweden; my mom is Norwegian and my dad is from Finland. I had never been further north than Stockholm in Sweden and I was curious to see more of the countries my roots came from.

This is how I came up with the crazy idea to ski solo from North Cape, the northernmost point of Europe, to Sweden (approximately 620 miles). I had never skied, slept in a tent in wintertime, or navigated before. I had six months to learn everything about winter in the Arctic, get sponsors to afford the equipment I needed, and drag car tires on Maroubra Beach in Sydney to get fit and build the right muscles. It was very important for me to talk to other people who had done similar things and to get advice. I have a lot of respect for nature and was very aware of how a little mistake could end up in disaster. I was going to cross Finnmarksvidda, a large plateau in northern Norway that is called the last wilderness of Europe, where temperatures can be as low as minus 40 degrees in winter and storms often hit the mountain plateau.

> I love to push my limits, but I also love just being in nature and enjoying the moment. For me there is no better place to be than in the mountains.

But for me the biggest challenge was the darkness. I started in February when the days were still short. I have been afraid of the dark since I was a child and couldn't think of anything worse than being alone in my tent in the dark, or, even worse, in a remote mountain cabin. I asked myself if this stupid fear was going to stop my dream. The darkness can't hurt me and is just something I have built up in my head. I had to step out of my comfort zone to deal with it.

I tried to focus on the more important parts of the expedition instead. I visualized a lot of situations before the trip, both bad and good. I could see myself pitching the tent in a storm, dealing with blisters on my feet, or feeling tired and lonely, but I could also see myself succeed on this journey and the amazing feeling I would have afterwards. I think this is a really good way to prepare yourself mentally for a big challenge. You will always go through tough times on expeditions and things will not always go as planned. I was told that if I can be "comfortable in an uncomfortable situation," I will be fine. If we want to grow as people, we must deal with the uncomfortable situations in life in order to develop.

I started my trip in February from North Cape. The days were short and temperatures went down to minus 35 degrees. There were winter storms and I skied for over a week without seeing any sign of life. But I also experienced the most amazing moments, waking up to sunrise in the east and a strong and bright moon in the west, and the Northern Lights dancing above my tent in the evenings. I felt so lucky that I got to experience this.

When I arrived in Sweden, the days were getting longer and warmer. Birds were singing and people were fishing on the lakes, and it hit me how much I had missed the spring and the contrasts of the different seasons. We take so much for granted in life and spending my first spring in Scandinavia after eight years in Sydney made me realize how fantastic and special the spring is.

After my ski expedition, I never returned to Sydney again. I booked a flight to Honningsvåg, near the start of the ski trip, which has just 3,000 inhabitants and is the northernmost city in Norway. I had dreamed about seeing mountains outside my doorstep and open ocean around me. This dream was coming true. I loved this place. It was so remote; it had extreme weather, endless wilderness, a lot of wildlife, and midnight sun, which also means polar nights in winter.

The following year I planned another solo expedition, this time to Siberia, to cross Lake Baikal from the southernmost to the northernmost point. Lake Baikal is the deepest freshwater lake in the world and the lake holds 20 percent of the world's fresh water. I walked 450 miles over the frozen lake over 14.5 days. I had many demanding and tough days on the lake, with temperatures down to minus 44 and strong winds that knocked me over on the ice, but I also had many beautiful moments, with incredible sunrises and sunsets. The ice was just amazing, so clear, and the sounds from it were both scary and fascinating.

When I got back to Norway after Lake Baikal it was time for a summer adventure together with my boyfriend, Stig-Rune, and our dog. We walked from the southernmost point of Norway home to North Cape. We spent 102 days walking 1,640 miles, spending most nights in our tent. We walked mainly through mountain terrain and wow, Norway has so many beautiful mountain areas to explore. I really enjoyed having company this time. Stig-Rune and I are a good match when we are hiking. We can both push on for long days when we need to; we had good routines in the tent and laughed a lot. I know many people saw it as a real test for us to spend so much time together, living in a small tent and pushing ourselves every day. We never saw it as a problem. Stig-Rune cooked dinner every night, while I wrote short blog posts and made some notes from the day, which I saved on my phone so I could easily copy them and do an update on my website once a week. When we pitched the tent, we had the same routines every single day. I think this is important to avoid small conflicts and it's always good to communicate with each other.

I love to push my limits, but I also love just being in nature and enjoying the moment, maybe fishing, sitting in front of a fire, or looking at a really good view with good company and good food. For me there is no better place to be than in the mountains.

Being out on longer expeditions has made me appreciate the things we take for granted in our daily life, like having access to a normal toilet, sleeping in a warm bed, taking a shower, wearing clean clothes, or going to the supermarket and choosing the day's food. These are the simple things that become luxuries on an expedition. They have also taught me to not get frustrated when the unexpected happens. Imagine finding out you've walked in the wrong direction for two hours, or maybe forgetting

*next page left* **Skiing and ice fishing in Karasjok, Norway, early on the season.**

*next page right, top left and bottom* **Camp spot from a 60-mile-long ski expedition on Sværholt Peninsula in Finnmark, Norway. A remote peninsula known for the harsh weather conditions in the area.** *top right* **A day from a 60-mile-long crossing of Finnmarksvidda on skis in bad weather early on the season.**

Easter trip on skis in Repvågstranda near my home in Finnmark, Norway.

ARC'TERYX
www.acapulka.co

Being out on longer expeditions has made me appreciate the things we take for granted in our daily life, like having access to a normal toilet, sleeping in a warm bed ... something at a cabin you just stayed the night at and having to walk back, or some of your equipment breaking. A normal reaction is to get upset and frustrated, but it won't help you to waste energy on it. Instead, you must deal with it and try to repair your equipment, or if you have walked the wrong way, you have to turn around and walk back. I can promise that a bad mood won't help at all. Remember, when things goes wrong or you have tough times in the mountains, that's when the best stories are created. If everything goes smoothly, you will never have anything fun to come back and tell everyone.

*left* **My playground just over a mile from my house in Honningsvåg, Norway.**

*top* **Trail running near the North Cape on a famous rock called Kirkeporten. Kirkeporten is a natural rock formation. Through it, you can look over the Mefjord to the North Cape, with its renowned North Cape Horn. In pre-Christian times, Kirkeporten and the North Cape Horn were both traditional Sami places of sacrifice.**

*top* Playful winter days together with Storm, my English pointer dog who comes along on most of my adventures.
*bottom* A stop to soak in the beautiful view and dry my top when hiking the length of Norway.
*opposite* Trail running on Magerøya island, Norway, in late spring near my home.

# AMANDA SPERAW
# THE NOMADIC MAMA

*We watched a short documentary about a couple who renovated a school bus. After that, we lay in bed talking about how we wished we could do it—which turned into, "Maybe we can."*

I am a nature-loving mama of two with another one on the way, and I live full-time in a tiny home on wheels. My husband and I started this adventure when our first baby was just a couple of months old. My husband was passionate about his job, but would basically leave the house when our son was waking up and return after his bedtime. Our family was missing out on lots of togetherness, which we desperately craved. We were both really starting to lose it, even though we had what seemed like the American Dream.

One day, we watched a short documentary on YouTube about a couple who built a "skoolie" (a renovated school bus that has been made into a home), traveled in it, and enjoyed all sorts of adventures on the road. After that, we lay in bed talking about how we wished we could do it—which turned into, "Maybe we can." We did the math and realized that with this type of lifestyle we could work less and actually save more. A few weeks later we bought our bus, sight unseen, on a government auction site and got to work.

Our first couple of years on the bus were fully nomadic. When we decided to jump into this way of living we sold *everything*, including our house and car. We mainly lived off those savings and investments and also had some odd jobs here and there that we could mostly do remotely. We traveled all over the country—from Key West to Olympic National Park in the Pacific Northwest. The three of us swam in crystal-clear oceans and rivers, and relaxed in as many hot springs as we could find along the way. I wore my baby on the longest hikes I've ever done, in almost every single state. We've followed autumn foliage down coastlines, all on our own time. We got to fully appreciate places we never would have visited had they not been along the way to somewhere else. One of the times that happened was when we found ourselves captivated by a herd of wild horses on the rolling hills of Theodore Roosevelt National Park in North Dakota. Another highlight was wearing my sleeping son while climbing the Beehive Trail in Acadia National Park, Maine.

During those years of traveling, we'd always hear, "I could never live the way you do," whether it be from a total stranger or a close family member. The truth was, we usually felt the same way about their lives. We never go all deep when people voice their opinions. Life would be so boring if everyone was the same. But because we lived the way we did, our kids got precious time with two full-time parents. Building our relationship with them made every sacrifice worth it. We lived in a "confined" space, but we were able to follow fair weather and spend almost every day outside. We ate healthier, stayed active outdoors, and were all around much happier than if we were living a "traditional" lifestyle.

We always had the goal to see what we could see, while being on the lookout for a new place to settle down—somewhere that had mountains, water, community, and sunshine! We didn't have a timeframe, but when we came to our mountain town in southwest Colorado, we knew we had found home. Thanks to our decision to convert a skoolie, we were able to buy land and have a place to live while we build

**With my son, Ezra, on a hike in Glacier National Park, Montana.**

**Traveling with kids can seem daunting, but once you get out there and get into the routine it is just so worth it.**

our A-frame. When that project is through (or maybe before), the goal is to convert something smaller than a 40-foot bus so we can still travel.

Bus life with kids doesn't come without its struggles. There is just so much that goes into off-grid living. When one thing isn't working, it makes life exponentially more difficult. It's not like in your typical house where you flip a switch and things work. There's solar power levels to consider, propane to hook up, water tanks to fill, ALWAYS dishes to wash, bedsheets way below my standards of cleanliness, and mice constantly getting into things. We've had water lines freeze and burst and break appliances. We've had issues on issues with the composting toilet. We've had a tire blow in the middle of nowhere when it was over 100 degrees out. It's hard not to let the little things get to you. It can be stressful finding a new spot to park while on the move, or when you're on the road and packages come late and need to be left behind, or when the dang dogs eat random plants wherever you go and get sick all over the bus.

There are honestly days when I am just tired of it all. But soon after, I am usually able to remind myself that these sacrifices come with great rewards. My son was able to build so much character on our travels throughout North America. Our children (and ourselves) will have a beautiful home in the mountains because of how we are living now. Our family spends so much more time outdoors than we used to because we get to travel to amazing places in our own home.

When things go wrong it's a challenge for us all. My husband and I were high-school sweethearts and have been each other's best friends since we were 16. We have practically grown up together and know each other best out of anyone in the world. To be brutally honest, I don't think our relationship would withstand this alternative lifestyle if it didn't have that solid foundation. When one thing goes wrong on the bus, it always seems like a domino effect, with more problems following in tow. It's not all sunshine and rainbows, but we both have an understanding that these experiences and tests are strengthening our marriage in the long run.

That being said, I wouldn't have changed our experience. Although I much prefer traveling in the bus to being in one spot, I know it's what needs to be done for my kids to have the best possible future. And traveling a bunch is going to happen again—I'm too addicted now. Traveling with kids can seem daunting, but once you get out there and get into the routine and figure out how to simplify it, it is just so worth it. There's nothing like the memories I have of the magical places I've been to with my family. Of my little boy, a fearless toddler, leaping into his daddy's arms in glacial Montana waters. Of my baby daughter, carried on my back, holding onto wildflowers as we climbed toward a summit in Colorado.

Maybe my babies won't remember these adventures. Probably not—they are so very young. But maybe they are building their character anyway. Maybe it's good they get more fresh air and less screens, and that a respect for nature and appreciation for discovery and exploration are becoming part of their very being. And maybe the photographs and mom and dad's recollections will be just what they need in the future. They might not quite remember these experiences, but maybe that's not the point.

*top* **Homeschool preschool on the bus.**

*bottom left* **Arts and crafts at the kids' table.**

*bottom right* **Boondocking in Southwest Colorado.**

*next page left* **Sequoia National Park, California.**

*previous page top left* **Southwest Colorado.**

*previous page top right* **Snowy day in Iowa.**

*previous page bottom* **Shenandoah National Park, Virginia.**

**Jumping into freezing waters at Glacier National Park, Montana.**

MT3754bA

**Our bus has taken us to the most beautiful mountain ranges, desert landscapes, and tropical beaches in the United States.** *top left* **Pregnant in Southwest Colorado.** *top right* **BLM land near Sedona, Arizona.** *bottom* **Clearwater, Florida.** *right* **Play on the bus.**

These are the days

*left* **River play in North Carolina.** *top* **Playalinda Beach, Florida.** *bottom left* **Kitchen organization on the bus.** *bottom right* **Gulf Islands National Seashore.**

# ALIENOR LE GOUVELLO
# THE HORSE TREKKER

*Riding solo with three horses across Australia from south to north is the most challenging and life-changing expedition I could have undertaken.*

*"He who would be free must not conform"*—Oscar Wilde

Oscar Wilde spoke to my wild heart at the age of 17, when I did not fit the mold of my private Parisian school. I made the bold decision to leave my home and move to India. It was the beginning of a life seeking the surprises that only adventure can bring.

I started an internship in photojournalism because I knew one thing: I wanted to travel. If it wasn't for dengue fever I might have traveled to Rajasthan on horseback, which I was passionate about. Fast forward 20 years, and now, at 37, I look back and reflect on the fact that although for a lot of that time I thought my life had no direction, it did. Being a free spirit took me to some of the most remote places of the world and fed my hunger for adventure and seeking new worlds. And in an unconventional way I fitted into every world I encountered. Twelve years on and off of working with indigenous youth in remote central Australia taught me so much about resilience and being at one with nature. So did every adventure I undertook on horseback or motorbike through Mongolia, Siberia, Eastern Europe, India, or Brazil. Although those expeditions were extremely tough at times, they were so rich. Rich in people, rich in culture and nature. People are always a big part of adventures, and a beautiful part, but the call of nature has been the common denominator in my expeditions.

Riding solo with three horses across Australia from south to north for 3,312 miles is the most challenging and life-changing expedition I could have undertaken. Being on the road with the horses and my dear dog, Fox, for 13 months enabled the most profound and deep connection with nature, and especially with my animals. My horses and my dog became my family. We were in complete harmony with nature, traveling engine-free. They gave me a sense of belonging and connection deeper than many I had experienced with humans. That bond is what got me through to the end as I battled with illness and had a couple of stints in hospital. I contracted Ross River fever, a tropical fever passed on by an insignificant mosquito that almost stopped me in my tracks after 10 months on the road and over 2,500 miles. Ross River is a debilitating illness that affects your joints and gives you chronic fatigue. The pain in my joints was excruciating. I disregarded the hospital doctor's advice to postpone my expedition for a few months and took high doses of painkillers and anti-inflammatories to get through each day. I woke up in the middle of the night to dose up on medication so I could function when I had to get up. My wrists and my ankles were the worst affected parts. I couldn't walk anymore, but I used to walk at least a third of the trekking day to relieve my horses and stretch my legs. When I'd get off, the pain of landing on the ground was such that I'd always let out a scream. My horses knew; they were amazingly patient with me. My actions were slow and clunky. Everything took a lot longer in pain—packing up the camp, loading the horses—and every day I felt like I had to move mountains. When I made it to camp I'd crash for a couple of hours, broken, unable to move. After pushing through for six weeks, violating my body, I contracted an infection called golden staphylococcus on my foot and leg. It's a nasty infection

**A stopover at a dam for a much-needed drink. I couldn't carry water for three horses and myself so when it presented itself we would never miss the opportunity.**

I made the bold decision to leave my home and move to India. It was the beginning of a life seeking the surprises that only adventure can bring.

which, if left untreated, can lead to deep, painful abscesses or infection of the blood, joints, and bones. After ignoring it for two weeks, with throbbing pain in my foot and leg, I ended up in hospital for a second time. I was on IV antibiotics for five days and had areas of my skin surgically removed, only just dodging infection to the joints and bones. Again I disregarded the doctor's advice to rest and left the hospital with my wounded leg in a plastic bag to get back on my horses and cross crocodile-infested rivers. I was only a week from finalizing my 13-month expedition at Cooktown, and nothing was going to stop me.

When I wrote my book *Wild at Heart*, every journalist had the same question that used to irritate me a lot: "What made you do this?" I used to say "Why not?" Why not undertake these adventures? Why does it need a deep and profound answer? Why do women need to undertake such adventures in order to "find

*left* **The spectacular rainforest makes me feel so small.**

*top* **It's hard not to become emotional when we near the end of our journey. I thank my heroes who have supported me throughout our trek.**

themselves"? That saying used to make me cringe. But the truth is, I hadn't really reflected on it. I just followed a call, an intuition. There was a much more profound answer, I just hadn't unraveled it yet—it took a further five years and some personal therapy for me to see it. After every expedition, I mentally crash, and especially after this one. An expedition like this overtakes your life. From the second you start planning to the moment it ends, it consumes you with its intensity and demands—logistics, survival skills—and the absolute sheer determination to make it to the end. Then, when it's over, there's the thought, "What next?" In my case it was either straight into another adventure or back into social work in remote indigenous communities. Both are all-consuming and offer no time to process.

Becoming a mother and slowing down for the first time in my life, as excruciating as it seemed at times, has allowed me that time to reflect on and process my adventures. Living with my child on a 2,300-square-mile cattle property, as romantic as that sounds, was extremely isolating, especially with a partner who works away from home. To help me through the struggle, I acquired two new wild horses to tame. I wanted to win their trust in the gentlest way possible and started learning and being mentored in a technique called liberty training, which involves working with horses in a way that they are free to participate in or not. The first step of liberty training is sitting in contemplation with the horse, with zero expectations, just being around them in a meditative state. This experience had a very powerful impact on me. It taught me patience, connection, and gratitude. It was the combination of my 13-month trek with the horses and this profound training experience that led me to study equine-assisted mental health and realize the healing power of nature and animals, especially horses. It has been a fascinating journey of self-discovery and growth. I'd always thought I was just a rebellious child and teenager, but through my therapy journey, I've come to understand my early childhood trauma. I sought refuge in animals and nature—that was my safe place. This awareness has brought peace and helped me understand the driving force of my adventures with animals and in nature.

**Over 13 long and gruelling months I traveled 3,312 miles from the south to the north of Australia with my three horses, Roxanne, River, and Cooper. Cat Vinton, an English photographer, joined us for a portion of the journey, observing and capturing the bond between me and my companions. I am so grateful to Cat for these memories of both the incredible highs of the trek, and the challenging lows.**

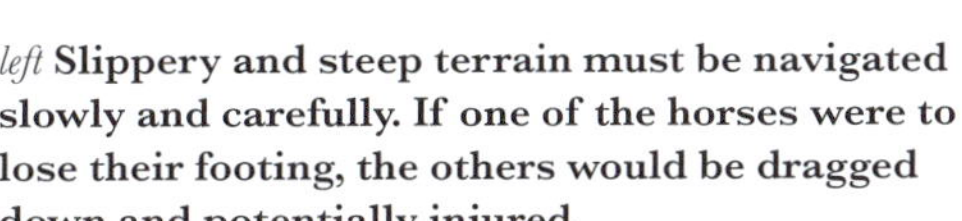

*left* **Slippery and steep terrain must be navigated slowly and carefully. If one of the horses were to lose their footing, the others would be dragged down and potentially injured.**

*top* **Traveling for 13 months and sharing camp life with my horses was really special. I got to know every intricate detail of each of their characters.**

*bottom* **The only huge downfall of the trail for a French person was the food. I could only carry really boring dry food.**

Through equine therapy I have found a vocation that combines my two passions: social work and horses.

Adventures challenge us. The adversity that we confront on expeditions calls upon inner reserves that would never be required in the comfort of everyday life. You find out what you're really made of. Adventures with horses offer something more—their profound healing power. Their hypersensitivity and ability to remain in harmony provides a mirror to the souls they interact with. Now when people ask "What made you ride horses across Australia?" I can answer "The challenge, and the opportunity to connect with horses and nature."

**Getting my saddle bags' weight even was crucial to ensure it wouldn't create pressure points on my horses' backs. A pack saddle is a dead weight on a horse and works against them. Their wellbeing was my top priority.**

*next page left* **Brumbies, considered a pest by the Australian government, are inquisitive and big-hearted animals. I shared a bond with my three companions that is unlike anything else.** *right* **Our path snakes through many outback stations and I often need to undo a fence when there are no gates. My players allow me to reassemble the fence afterwards.**

BAYER

*left* I am forever grateful for my companions' resilience and strength; they never failed me. *top* It's important to rest and allow our bodies to heal. *bottom* Gathering wood to make a fire for cooking and to bring comfort and collecting water in my bucket for camp and washing. *next page* Rocky terrain was hard on my horses' feet. I got off and walked for at least one third of each trekking day.

# BETHSHEBA BLANKEN
# THE SLOW TRAVELER

*As soon as I got into the outdoors, I felt like I had come home. All I wanted was to explore and be in nature as much as possible.*

I was born on a big plot of land surrounded by nature on a tiny island in the Caribbean called Curaçao. My hippie parents raised me and my five siblings in a minimalistic and holistic way connected with nature. For personal reasons, we had to move to a big city in the Netherlands when I was young. Although I got used to my new life quickly, I always struggled with fitting into the "normal" life. I remember calling myself a city girl once I grew up, but deep down I knew it wasn't my place and something was missing.

Day-to-day life in the Netherlands was too fast and overwhelming and I couldn't keep up (the gray climate also didn't help). I tried so hard but I often felt lost and struggled with depression as a teen and as an adult. After I graduated, I started working as a make-up artist, but as much as I loved my job, I quickly started to feel like this life wasn't for me. I decided to quit my job and sell 80 percent of my stuff, and three months later I said goodbye to my old life to pursue something I secretly dreamed of: traveling around the world and living in different countries.

I have been traveling slowly for over four years and my life has changed completely! As soon as I got into the outdoors, I felt like I had come home. My adventurous spirit awoke and all I wanted was to explore more and be in nature as much as possible. I found out that I wasn't a city girl at all and could care less about wearing nice clothes and make-up. I realized my parents were pretty badass for getting away from society and trying to raise their kids in a minimalistic way connected with nature. I guess the apple did not fall far from the tree after all.

Slow travel is more about the journey itself than the destination. It's the art of slowing down in a fast-paced world and getting back to the root of why we travel. It's looking for a richer, more meaningful experience along the way rather than just doing a whirlwind tour of an entire country in a short amount of time and only visiting the top to-do's. It's about interacting with the place while you're there, immersing yourself in the culture. Slow travel encouraged me to be a more mindful and responsible traveler and is also the reason why I tend to spend a longer amount of time in countries. I want to fully immerse myself in the cultures, see how locals spend their daily lives, and find out whether I can become one of them by living in the country and exploring off the beaten path.

Over the past four years, I have lived and traveled in a van in Australia, journeyed around Southeast Asia, driven across Vietnam on a motorcycle, learned to scuba dive in Thailand, climbed volcanoes in Indonesia, fallen in love with the great outdoors and lived in my minivan in New Zealand, converted and lived in a small panel van in Europe, and recently made my move to the Portuguese island of Madeira.

Life on the road is truly amazing and even though it is a bit over-romanticized by social media, I love it! Waking up in the morning surrounded by nature, being outside so much, the freedom it gives, and the way you take life at a slower pace without needing much is what makes it all worth it for me. While living in New Zealand I fell in love with the great outdoors after one of my roommates took me on a hike. I had never

**A refreshing afternoon dip at Seealpsee in Switzerland, after eight hours of hiking.**

## I got tired of having to beg people or wait for others to be able to join me, so I decided to go solo.

backpacked before or hiked, other than going up volcanoes or to viewpoints in Asia. But after that one hike I was immediately hooked and started to use all my days off to explore the trails.

Being in the outdoors shapes me in many ways: It calms me down from the everyday hustle and bustle and reminds me to appreciate all the beautiful things in life, both big and small. It shows me I'm capable of so much more than I thought. It's the place I truly feel the happiest, no matter whether I'm covered in dirt and sweat, haven't showered for days, and have only eaten some energy bars and dried food. I'll take it over any fancy trip or restaurant.

My friends and ex-partner weren't as excited about slow travel as I was. I got tired of having to beg people or wait for others to be able to join me, so I decided to go solo. It was a bit scary at first, as you often don't have phone service on the trails, and I had little experience in the wilderness. I started with short trails and soon felt comfortable enough to go on longer day hikes and even solo overnight hikes. I had no clue what I was doing at first, but I was stubborn, learned as I went, and made many mistakes about what to bring. I searched blogs and YouTube and every time I stayed in a mountain hut I would observe what other hikers brought with them and copy their hacks on my next adventure.

I soon realized I was a bit of an outcast. I often get funny looks on trails and in huts. Luckily, in most cases, it's friendly faces and I don't focus on negativity. Whenever I feel uncomfortable I always try to remind myself that I belong there just as much as anyone else. I might be the first Black woman they see there, but I'm hoping to inspire many others, and I definitely won't be the last. They'd better get used to it!

I do get scared at times and I take safety precautions. I always check reviews of camp grounds, lock my van at night, and trust my intuition. Whenever a place, person, or situation feels off I leave. I pin every spot I sleep in Google Maps, partly so I remember but also so my route is traceable in case anything goes wrong. I tell others if I'm going on an adventure and when I will be back, so they can raise the alarm if I haven't returned before that time. I also don't often go solo backpacking on lesser-known trails in rural areas or wilderness, especially not if there are hunters around. Something about being a young Black

*left* **Adelboden, Switzerland.** *right* **Solo hike to Schäfler mountain hut in Switzerland. I stayed the night and celebrated my 26th birthday surrounded by the beautiful Alpstein mountains.**

TERREX

woman staying alone in a mountain hut or rural areas with armed men doesn't feel like a situation I want to be in. Being a woman is one thing, but in the back of my mind, it still sits with me that someone could be racist and I would be out there alone. However, doing things I wouldn't usually do and going to places where I usually wouldn't belong gives me excitement and a feeling of accomplishment, so I continue to push myself further out of my comfort zone, even if it's by doing smaller things like camping alone instead of staying in a mountain hut.

I would love to get into more mountain sports. Maybe one day I'll climb the high peaks in Nepal to test myself and inspire others. No matter our background or when we start, we—the outsiders—truly belong everywhere!

**Enjoying the morning sun while hiking the Cabo da Roca to Azenhas do Mar coastal trail in Portugal.**

These moments alone in nature are where I feel the happiest and most alive. I immediately feel more relaxed and at ease while out in nature: I'm able to let go of my worries and be in the moment, enjoying the simple things in life.

*top* **Mt Brown Hut, New Zealand.**

*bottom* **My first time sleeping in a tent by myself. It was a bit lonelier than sleeping in a hut as there are usually other backpackers, but it was still a fun and empowering experience. Limmersee, Switzerland.**

*right* **Grimsel Pass, Switzerland.**

*next page left* **Steinsee, Switzerland.** *right* **Roys Peak, New Zealand.**

*top* **I came across this road while traveling and felt like it represented my journey, full of twists and turns leading me to all different kinds of directions I never expected myself to go in. But it's in these detours that I found myself.** *right* **Bachalpsee, Switzerland.**

*left* **Bachalpsee, Switzerland.** *right* **Queenstown, New Zealand. Traveling isn't always fun and games. Dealing with a break-up, anxiety, and feeling burned out from work without having my support system near me was so tough. I decided to go back to the Netherlands and travel or move somewhere closer to home.**

# LIBBY DELANA
# THE MORNING WALKER

*This simple act, a morning walk, has become a daily ritual that has transformed my life.*

I started going for a walk every morning in 2011, because I realized that a key piece of who I am wasn't part of my life in a meaningful way: Time in the outdoors. I am nourished in the outdoors; it's where I am inspired and most creative. Being outdoors is my happy place. It is where I spent my childhood and found a true sense of freedom. It is where I found myself. So I committed to going for a walk every morning for a month and here I am 26,000 miles later (the circumference of the earth), never having missed a day. Walking has been my way back to myself, a practice that brings me home. I have never regretted a walk, never. This simple act, a morning walk, has become a daily ritual that has transformed my life.

I am a believer that we have to make time, not find time, for the things that make us us. The outdoors is essential to who I am, and I believe it's essential to who we all are. In my case, life had become getting in cars, sitting in meetings, running errands, producing—and completing—to do lists. I realized that what made me me was no longer intimately part of my days. Looking back, the feeling of being overwhelmed by errands, conference calls, shoulds, have-to's, and endless expectations had overtaken me. I had lost my footing, my grounding. I needed to get back to a bigger sense of purpose—beginning with a fundamental intimacy with the earth.

I have come to believe that walking is essential medicine—for us, for our communities, and for the earth. Why is it essential medicine for the earth? Because I believe that unless we are vibrantly connected to the seasons, the weather, and the natural world, we don't have the instinct to protect, listen to, and honor the earth—and as a result we also don't protect, listen to, or honor each other.

Up at 5 a.m., out the back door, often the same 5–10 mile loop. I walk past the same barn, on the same path, next to the same river, with the same headwind around that last turn. This conscious repetition is a form of meditation, designed with intentional familiarity. It's almost as if I could do it blindfolded. In fact, some days, on the back stretch, I close my eyes while walking for 10, 20, 30, 40 steps. Do I really know where I am?, I wonder. Am I listening to my gut, my body, to the wisdom embedded in this moment? The mindlessness of the route itself brings with it a sense of mindfulness. I am not focused on the route or my steps but instead on this moment. This breeze on my face. This joyous birdsong. This breath in. This breath out. This breath in. This breath out.

I start many walks with an intention, question, idea, or concern, and by the end of the walk, I have held space for it for long enough that we have made friends with each other. We have rumbled, we have danced, and we have said hello and goodbye. My thoughts roll, change, and expand while I walk, sometimes with every step. There is great power for me in the clarifying energy of a walk. I don't really know what I feel or think unless I move. To add motion to emotion is an essential reason I walk.

To honor this process, I started taking pictures on my walk. Not only was this simple act a tool of accountability but also, as an art director, my language is primarily visual. Snapping a photograph of the same dilapidated barn day after day taught me to see again, not simply look. It made me really see

**Plum Island, Massachusetts. It was late summer and very, very still. Just beyond the edge of this path is the Atlantic Ocean, which was poetically calm.**

I am a believer that we have to make time, not find time, for the things that make us us.

*left* **Newburyport, Massachusetts. The first snowfall. I was the only one in this forest this morning. It felt like such a privilege.**

*top left* **I am happiest outdoors, always have been. Fall, Newburyport, Massachusetts.** *top right* **I walk these boardwalks at least once a week. The beauty of walking the same path is to see the variation of each day, each season, each moment.**

something as if for the first time each day. Over and over again, I was amazed at how much I had overlooked. What else had I missed all these years?

After finishing a walk, I began posting the pictures on Instagram as a way to keep a record of these moments. It wasn't for anyone else, it was for me. A visual diary. A history. A captured moment. A record of the unexpected snowstorm, the foggy sunrise, the lineup of ravens on the roof, the rain pouring off my hat brim. It was also a way to honor the gratitude I felt for being able to walk. I do not take it for granted that I am able to do this each day. I have the time (my kids are grown), I have the physical ability, I feel safe, I live in a beautiful area of the world. I am often overwhelmed with gratitude and acknowledge my privilege, and these photos are the visual reminder of that daily dose of gratitude.

I do not take it for granted that I am able to do this each day.

This daily micro-practice has informed life in ways I would never have expected, from new friendships (started by a simple comment on a photo) to collaborations with incredible makers and doers, and perhaps—most importantly—to a profound awareness of our connectedness. Now, 11 years later, we have a small, loving community of people who walk together, even though we may be on the other side of the world from each other. I often walk with a friend who lives halfway around the world. We each go for a walk in our own community, then we check in afterward to see what we learned, what we were feeling, and tell each other how much we care about one another. It feels as if we were walking together because we were each thinking about the other as we walked.

It has turned out that this is my most valuable processing time. I often have something to work on when I head out the door. It may be about trying to figure out a creative challenge at work, or a personal issue that I need space to understand. This moving meditation creates the space and pace I often need to understand a situation. Here I am in the place I am most comfortable, and I can allow my thoughts, my feelings, my brain to deconstruct and then reframe an issue. It turns the walk into both an escape and a focused, intentional act. It is the key to my operating system. It is my act of radical self-care.

Good things always happen on a walk. And I am always grateful, never sorry, when I get home. Today, my daily walk is a sacred act, the kindest gift I can give myself. It is perhaps the kindest gift I can give the world.

I have recently been considering: "Can a daily morning walk save the world?" This is a question I have been walking with this past week. Here is the reason I ask this question: I feel as if I have learned some very significant lessons while walking, all of which have fundamentally changed the way I see, feel, and understand the world. I think these lessons are available to us all, and they have the potential to heal, help, save, shift, and inspire our world toward a more whole and kinder path. So the answer is: Yep. Yes. It sure can.

So join me. Take a walk. Consider going every day for 30 days and see what happens. Happy walking!

*left* **Cape Neddick Light, York, Maine. There is something about the Maine air that feels so essential. It is briny and sweet all at once. Maine is a very special and grounded place.**

*right* **The outdoors is who I am. I often feel lost indoors, but never outdoors. Fall, Newburyport, Massachusetts.**

*left* December, Norfolk, Connecticut. This elegant stone wall was tucked in between the tree line. It is one of the most beautiful things I have ever seen. *top* Hilo, Hawai'i. I was on a photoshoot for work and wandered away from the set to find this endless path to everywhere. *bottom* Christmastime, Norfolk, Connecticut. I went out for my morning walk before everyone else had begun their day. The house was quiet. It was even quieter outside.

# CAL MAJOR
# THE SUP ADVENTURER

*I began to learn how much I loved the rawness and unpredictability of ocean adventures.*

When I was 18, before starting vet school, I learned to scuba dive on Australia's Great Barrier Reef, and I fell deeply in love with the ocean and the animals in it. Throughout college, I surfed and dived at every opportunity, and knew I wanted to dedicate my life to protecting the ocean and its creatures. After I graduated as a vet, surfing, stand up paddleboarding (SUP), and having adventures around the coast became the most powerful antidote to long, stressful days in the clinic, and my connection to the sea deepened even further.

The more I explored the beaches and ocean around where I lived in the southwest of England, the more horrified I became by the amount of plastic waste I was finding. It was on every beach, even the tiniest, most remote coves that were only accessible by water. I felt compelled to do something about it, so I set out to call attention to it in the best way I knew how—through adventure. I decided to take on a stand up paddleboarding challenge, to paddle 300 miles around the entire coast of Cornwall, highlighting the trash I found, and bringing to light positive solutions. My journey would take me three weeks, paddling six to eight hours a day. I expected endless hours of sunshine and dolphins; I soon learned that SUPing in the UK, even in summer, did not guarantee a sun tan and a six pack, as I was faced with gale-force winds, overhead waves, rain, and fog! But I also began to learn how much I loved the rawness and unpredictability of ocean adventures and wild camping, and how much more powerful my messages were when seen through the lens of adventure.

The following year I SUPed around the Isle of Skye in Scotland, a remote and wild place, and found enormous amounts of waste on every beach I visited. On one such beach I came across a cow who had swallowed part of a fishing net, the other part hanging out of her mouth. I filmed what I could, and a clip of this poor cow went viral, opening my eyes to film as a powerful method of storytelling. My partner and I made a film about the expedition, which traveled to film festivals and schools around the world to further educate people on how ubiquitous and invasive the ocean plastic pollution problem is, and to inspire more conversations and positive change. I returned from the Isle of Skye with a heightened sense of how noisy and stressful life is in our busy towns and societies, and immediately craved a return to the wilds, where everything was quiet and real.

The next year, 2018, I set a new Guinness World Record as the first person to SUP the 1,000 miles from Land's End to John O'Groats, the whole length of the UK. It took two months of paddling day and night whenever the tides and winds allowed, and was by far the hardest thing I'd ever done. I made enormous crossings, often several miles out to sea, rounded infamous headlands through crazy tidal races, and camped on deserted beaches. At the time, I was grieving the loss of a close friend to suicide, and the solitude and companionship of the ocean provided an enormous amount of solace. I spoke with communities around the coast who were active in tackling plastic pollution in their local areas, and compared it to inland waterways where the awareness wasn't as apparent. I began to realize that the—often missing—crucial first step in protecting a

**Elgol, Isle of Skye, Scotland, shortly after becoming the first woman to circumnavigate the island by SUP in 2017, solo: one of my most formative and empowering expeditions. I was thrown in at the deep end with a huge learning curve ahead of me.**

finisterre

The more I explored the beaches and ocean around where I lived in the southwest of England, the more horrified I became by the amount of plastic waste I was finding.

place is having a personal connection to it, and that I could talk to people until I was blue in the face about the marine litter crisis, but without an understanding of what the sea meant to them personally, it would likely fall on deaf ears. This felt like a profound realization, and I took a turn in my campaigning to focus on how we can all individually, and collaboratively, reconnect to the sea. I was experiencing for myself the mental health benefits that being on or near blue spaces holds, which I had heard about time and time again from those I met around the coast. I realized that reconnecting our societies to nature was for the benefit of people and the planet we inhabit.

I set up the charity Seaful to help reconnect people to nature, in particular our oceans. To this day, we take mostly young people to blue spaces, for them to experience them, play, and learn about the ecosystems and their roles in our lives. The

*left* **Elgol, Isle of Skye, Scotland.**

*top* **Arctic Circle, Norway—one of the most spectacular, and coldest, places I've ever paddled.**

reactions have been incredible: awe, wonder, and surprise at the smallest of things. We snorkel, rockpool, and SUP, among other ocean-based activities, and incorporate mindfulness into all our sessions. We specifically aim our activities at those who may not have been to the sea before, or who have not had the opportunities to do the activities on offer. We also make films to further inspire and educate our next generation, telling the ocean's stories. Watching seeds being sown is truly magical and a great privilege to witness.

In 2021 I paddled around my favorite country in the world—Scotland. I set off on my SUP from outside the SEC in Glasgow, where a few months later the COP26 international climate talks would be held. I paddled for two and a half months around Scotland to the last harbor on the east coast. This took in the infamous Cape Wrath and the unforgiving north coast of Scotland, which was even more challenging and wild than I'd expected it to be. The ocean plays an enormous role in all of our lives, and we're in the midst of a global climate and biodiversity crisis. Our planet is 70 percent covered in water, and the ocean produces the oxygen in every second breath we breathe! It's home to incredible ecosystems, awe-inspiring animals, and carbon-capturing, oxygen-producing plants. And yet, to so many people around the globe, it's out of sight and out of mind. Not just its beauty and the wonderful creatures and life underwater, but the destruction that's befalling it. All of us rely on a healthy ocean for our lives and our health. But many of us are blind to this, and the threats facing it. So my trip was all about showing what's under the surface, from the tiniest crustaceans to the largest apex predators, and exploring our connection to the seas.

I could not have asked for a more immersive and eye-opening experience. On my journey I saw dolphins, sea eagles, and gannets galore. I paddled through rafts of puffins and guillemots, swam through seagrass and all the life associated with it, and caught my first glimpses of maerl—a small, intricate coralline algae that forms the base of the inshore ecosystems. However by far the most special experience I've ever had on the water was one gray morning in the Northwest Highlands. I'd been paddling since dawn and was utterly exhausted, struggling even to kneel on my board, let alone stand. Just as my energy hit an all-time low, I heard a "pfft" behind me. I turned around expecting to see dolphins, and instead saw three enormous jet-black fins, two of them 6 foot tall, heading straight towards me. Orca. Two males circled me while a female swam underneath my board, turning on her side as she did so and looking straight up at me. For a fraction of a second, I locked

**Rubha Hunish, Isle of Skye, Scotland. A dramatic turning point marking the beginning of the home stretch on my Isle of Skye circumnavigation. Huge imposing cliffs, whose waters are famed for their whales and eagles.**

STARBOARD
STARBOARD
Palm

*left* **Isle of Skye, with the Skye bridge in the distance behind me. This image was made into the poster for the award-winning film we made about that expedition—"Skye's the Limit."**

*top* **Senja, Norway. It was a dream come true to paddle underneath the Northern Lights.**

*right* **Ersfjordstranda, Norway, wading into icy water in the twilight, hoping my dry-trousers hold up!**

eyes with a killer whale. They swam away as quickly as they'd arrived, but their visit remains with me to this day. Their size, speed, and ability in the water was utterly terrifying and humbling, and it was by far the most unbelievably special encounter I've had in all my years paddleboarding.

Not all my encounters with wildlife were so positive. I experienced multiple encounters with wildlife entangled in fishing gear. One was a juvenile humpback whale, floating dead on the surface. Another was a beautiful gannet, whose injuries were mild and which I was fortunately able to release.

People often ask how I keep going when I'm out at sea, paddling all hours, day after day. I'm driven by purpose. The more time I spend out at sea, the more I experience what's there and the more deeply I care about its fate. The more wildlife encounters I have, the more magic and love I experience, and the more I feel duty bound to do everything in my power to protect the animals in our seas. The more I see underwater, the more awe and wonder I experience and the more passionate I feel about protecting our oceanic ecosystems from human damage. The more damage I see, the more impassioned I am to advocate for change. The more I realize how utterly privileged I am to have these experiences, the more determined I am to help the one in five children in the UK who have never been to the sea to experience it too. My adventures are crucial for telling stories, and I keep going because I believe that those stories desperately need to be told.

**Isle of Skye, the moment I finished my circumnavigation of this wild and dramatic island and paddled into the beach to be greeted by my mum and dad. I was delighted to return after two weeks of self-sufficiency, fierce winds and tides, and shocking discoveries.**

*top* **Near Lybster, Scotland, on the final stretch to John O'Groats. Little did I know what was awaiting me just up the coast.**

*top right* **Whitbeck, Cumbria, a very remote beach upon which tons of plastic had washed in.**

*bottom left* **"In a world where you can be anything, be kind."**

*bottom right* **Lombok, Indonesia, in my element.**

BE KIND

# MANDY SHAM
# THE NOMAD-ISH EXPLORER

*I'm a person who likes to document, a wanderer, a learner by sense and observation.*

I was 23, inhaling every last atom of thin air at 15,000 feet above sea level, climbing a mountain pass in the Himalayas with a water bottle that was frozen shut. The road, traversed now for days, was lit by starlight and little else. The distant headlamps of the others flickered like fireflies, appearing as if they ascended a staircase that led to the sky. By the time I stopped to rest, Nepal's vast emptiness shook me to speechlessness. I felt strange, standing so far away from where I might be in a different life. Feeling the primordial earth of a place that could only be reached either by days on foot, helicopter, or not at all. The beauty of hiking in near-silence to the ends of the world—with hardly the physique required for the task at hand—is knowing that it's an adventure you choose. Travel became the way for a lost and sad twenty-something to learn the value of that choice.

When I look back at the things that transformed my life, there are moments that shine iridescently—like being high up in the remote Nepali villages that breathe the air of a different time, climbing a giant prehistoric rock in the Namibian desert, and enjoying long, happy, wine-fueled nights in a bush camp. There are odd, singular moments—like sleeping for two nights on the massage bed of a hammam in the heart of Marrakech's medina, skiing on mud through a bamboo forest in northern Vietnam, and walking for hours through Maltese countryside, alone. Moments that delight, bore, and make me think "What?" My beating heart and alive body have done this, and I am the result.

**Self-portrait, inside a colorful home in Colonia Roma, Mexico City, on a sweet October day.**

Still, what I am—and the task of defining it—becomes increasingly alien with every passing year. The perennial fear as a writer is, ironically, committing memories to words, because doing so runs the risk of erasing the three-dimensionality of things. Once written, a memory is often thought of in the way in which it's already been expressed. The other details are likely to fade with time. The definition of self works in a similar way, in my view. I know I'm some things: a person who likes to document, a wanderer, a learner by sense and observation. It's drawn me to writing and taking photographs for a living. I love putting down roots as much as I enjoy challenging the limits of home as something physical. I'm a journalist by accident, then by choice.

But I haven't landed on the truth of what I'm about, or where I'll end up. Life seems intuitive at times, but at other times it feels chaotic and unknown. In a way, the ordeal of traveling through the smallest oasis towns in the middle of a desert or through winding and inaccessible mountain roads, only to hear someone voice the very same earthly doubts, is the great beauty of doing it at all.

The world is as grand as it is small. That's a lesson I've been taught many times but never tire of hearing. In Istanbul, the living relics of the Byzantine and Ottoman empires are overwhelming in every way. There is no way to deny my foreignness when I'm there, and I don't bother trying. The glittering trinkets and traditional sweets in the sprawling bazaars carry a secret I'll never know: an inter-generational heirloom, inseparable from anyone who has spent a lifetime walking down Istanbul's streets.

I know that going far—whether it's hitching a ride in Jordanian desert or camping by the side of a highway in Mozambique—is precisely a reminder of what I'm made of.

But then, of course, comes the small world: moments that bring you into the fold of a different yet oddly familiar life. In Turkey, it was partaking in a coffee fortune-telling ritual—seated at an old cafe among people who felt like good friends. On another occasion, I remember meeting an old acquaintance by complete coincidence, and sharing a decade's worth of small triumphs and doubts at a restaurant overlooking the Bosphorus. Looking at that line drawn between Europe and Asia, we talked about our complicated families, our mixed identities, and all the places we belonged.

It may be a product of my upbringing, but I have always felt foreign. My family moved intermittently between Hong Kong and Toronto. Even as they settled into suburban life, there were trips to the homeland—or to Chinese canteens, tucked away into small plazas—to make us feel at home again. It was possible to go a whole day speaking nothing but Cantonese. We were decent at Canadian life, too—shoveling snow from our driveway on hot-chocolate-fueled winters, and rollerblading down the cul-de-sac where we lived. Life was best when it was boring. Looking back, the neighborhood where I grew up was perfectly suited to us. It was a sleepy suburb filled with a kind of anxious diaspora. Everything and everyone was foreign, so nothing was.

But my childhood also taught me that everybody's food smelled—unapologetically, deliciously. My high school lunches were jerk chicken poutine and Hong Kong-style egg sandwiches. My family's love language has long been food: a plate of cut fruit to mend arguments, and a childhood filled with long hours at the dim sum table among relatives. Our small dinner table at home was a quiet one, but no one ever left the table when "dinner" was done. In spite of how we tried, language has never connected me to my parents in the same capacity food has. I am convinced that something as simple as the contents of a plate are what opened my door to the world. When I started traveling in earnest, an early trip to Vietnam brought me to the rice terraces of Sapa, where a friend and I trekked for two days, along with our guide Chi. At her home, Chi's family prepared a lunch by kettle and fire. The banana flower salad and fried beans were the most exquisite morsels of that entire trip. I learned they'd been cooked with nothing other than oil and salt, and it sparked something in my young and unknowing brain—the idea that something could taste so much like itself, harvested in local soil and cooked with wisdom over a small hearth.

That experience in Vietnam would repeat itself time and time again. It was the easiest way for countries to reveal themselves to me. In the mountains of Georgia, following an hours-long dinner brimming with garlic chicken and wine, the matriarch of the household brought me into her kitchen to show how she made khinkali—classic twisted, knobby dumplings stuffed with meat and Georgian spices. We ate past midnight, rummaging through her spice cabinet and chatting excitedly about mostly nothing. It's in situations like these, seated at dinner with strangers who become friends in the clearing of a plate, overwhelmed by a culture and language so far from my own, that I feel the most innate sense of belonging. There's no denying the sacredness of a table where people gather to eat, no matter where you are in the world. As someone who has long felt that home is elsewhere, travel has taught me I am the only thing I can hold onto.

With that knowledge, I know that going far—whether it's hitching a ride in Jordanian desert or camping by the side of a highway in Mozambique—is precisely a reminder of what I'm made of. I am confronted by my physicality on a mountain or a surfboard; I'm reminded of the fact I'm a woman of color, and all that entails in the places I visit. But it is, equally, a journey of human resilience and empathy. I am touched by the world's capacity for kindness and curiosity. I am all the experiences that have molded me.

*top* **The nomadic Maasai, on the sprawling plain of Tanzania. The savanna goes far further than the eye can see.**

*bottom left* **One could never tire of the long train journeys through Sri Lankan hill country—whether it's the lush greenery at every glance, the flow of passengers entering and departing at every stop, or the wallas ambling down the aisle with spiced lentil doughnuts and strong cups of chai.**

*bottom right* **Commuting in Mumbai. In a span of minutes the city waxes and wanes in density, exposing a world of neighbourhoods, fields, and packed urban areas.**

*next page* **You can almost smell it, the herbal scents, the ripening guavas, the frying oil. The aisles of merchants are enchanting in their organized disarray. Udaipur is exquisite in every sense.**

*top left* An improvised barber shop inside the labyrinthine, dense Dharavi slum in Mumbai. *top right* The beating heart of India can be found almost everywhere, but in markets it is especially potent: a language you don't need to speak to perceive, spelled out in a symphony of colors and aromas. *bottom* Captured on film, in my spiritual home. Hong Kong's harbour has an ancestral familiarity to it. There's an unspeakable allure to the waves, smelling of seaweed and rusting metal; the bright and insatiable skyline represents a city brimming with aspiration.

*previous page left* Sundown by the Arabian Sea. As the heat loses its grip, people begin to shift gears: a slower and more relaxed pace, as if to digest the frenetic comings and goings of the day. *previous page right* The Udaipur Palace in only a fraction of its splendour—a precious, ornate living monument, graced by the sea of visitors dressed in every imaginable color. *left* Mexico City: a place unmatched in its vibrancy and outward character. Every building's paint, whether fresh or peeling, reveals its stories. The streets feel more than walked on; they feel inhabited. *right* There is always such excitement that comes with passing by the train stations of the world. What lies beyond? Where are people going next? Imagination runs spectacularly when the wheels are in motion—transporting you to places you've never been, and keeping you there.

පිරිමි
විවේක කාමරය
ஆண்கள்
இளைப்பாறும் அறை
GENTS
REST ROOM

# MORGAN MATHERS
# THE UNDERWATER EXPLORER

*My parents gave me the name Morgan which I always find fitting, since it means "from the sea." I don't know if at the time they knew that it would have so much significance in my life.*

Before I introduce myself, let me take you into my world: It's a beautiful glassy morning and the water is crystal blue. After checking the conditions, we suit up and jump in the water. We load our spearguns by pulling the bands into our chest and then kick out to the grounds. From the surface we will examine the reef below us, looking for specific species of fish. Before you take a drop, you breathe up for a couple of minutes, bringing yourself to a calm relaxed state. After your last breath of air, you dive down and start equalizing the pressure in your ears. After about 30 feet you lose buoyancy, stop kicking, and start to free fall to the bottom. You will want to find a hiding spot, whether under a shelf or behind a boulder. Curious fish will start to swarm around you and create a commotion, alerting other bigger fish that there could be something around that they want in on. You will begin to fluff the sand, grunt, or scratch on rocks, while also scanning the environment around you. One of the best things about spearfishing is that it is selective hunting. You spot an elusive mu (bigeye emperor) in the distance and continue to hide your eyes, fluff, and scratch rocks. You feel the contractions in your chest become stronger and tighter. Just before you think about returning to the surface, the mu comes in closer, giving you a shot. You bring your gun forward, line up with the fish, and shoot. The gun kicks back and the shaft penetrates the fish. As you move to the surface, you experience a blissful feeling of success and hypoxia. When you bring up your catch, you get a closer look at how big your fish actually is. You take a moment for gratitude and appreciation. When we arrive at shore we will clean and scale our catch and put it on ice. Later that evening, we will spend our time preparing dinner and honoring our catch. Smiles, stories, and fish will be shared around the dinner table.

My parents gave me the name Morgan which I always find fitting, since it means "from the sea." I don't know if at the time they knew that it would have so much significance in my life. It almost seems as though my life in the water was predestined. I was born in Heidelberg, Germany, in 1998, while my dad was stationed overseas. Since we were an army family, every two years we would pack up our lives and move to the next place. Somehow we always found ourselves near a body of water. I grew up sailing, swimming, and snorkeling in Puerto Rico, Key West, the Chesapeake, the Jersey Shore, Puget Sound, and eventually Oahu, Hawai'i. There I felt the obsessive tug of the ocean, and spent all my free time between high school and college diving with my younger sister and friends. Navigating my way after school societal structures left me feeling disillusioned and unsatisfied; I could not envision living a normal nine-to-five. The only thing I knew to be fulfilling was my life underwater. I had to pursue my passion. At the age of 23, the ocean brought my fiancé and me together. We bonded over our love of the ocean, exploring, and creating underwater films. I then moved to the countryside on the island of Hawai'i to cultivate a farm and homestead with my fiancé and to spend my days diving in some of the most magical waters in the world. I continue to navigate life by following my heart, appreciating the simple things in life, and flowing with serene ocean tides.

**Sometimes my dreams will take me to underwater places. Even in my sleep I will be diving in caverns with insane skylights, swimming with orcas, or even spearfishing.**

From my very first catch I was absolutely hooked on spearfishing. It's given me a new sense of appreciation for my food, ecosystem, and ability to dive.

My diving journey has evolved throughout the years. When I first began to freedive I was motivated to swim through underwater lava tubes, exploring caves and admiring underwater topography. Putting myself through solid obstacles that I would have to complete in order to get back to air advanced my diving pretty quickly. When I swam into these underwater caves and tunnels I'd imagine they were underwater mansions, and I was a mermaid shopping for a house. The way sunlight dances through the cracks and cave fish dart in and out of the shadows is truly ethereal.

After what felt like swimming through every cave and tube on the island, I started diving for shells. Shells are brought by ocean swells. I found myself kicking out in the surf to collect the beautiful treasures the Pacific has to offer. I learned how to dance with the waves. Making a mistake or being greedy in this environment could end up with you tumbling across the reef back to shore. To collect these ocean jewels I had to dive in spots that typically were choppy, with white wash and an intense energy. I had to teach myself how to stay calm and breathe up at the surface with all this chaos around me if I wanted a chance to collect what was being guarded by the elements. I loved making crafts and jewelry with the shells I collected so I could admire them throughout the day and think of my adventures in the ocean. After obtaining a collection I could only previously have dreamed of, my diving journey evolved into another form of harvesting.

It wasn't until I met my fiancé, Perrin, that I developed an interest in spearfishing. Before his career in underwater film and photography, he was a professional spearfishing guide around the world. We spend most of our quality time together underwater. When we dived together he'd bring a speargun and catch a fish if the opportunity presented itself. Later that evening he'd prepare a sashimi plate or steamed fish for me. It was those meals that motivated me to learn how to catch fish. Although I had years of diving experience, I learned on my first three-prong mission that freediving and spearfishing are two different skills. I had the depth and the power to hold my breath, but I needed to work on my fish identification, body language, and how to read the fish. Learning the basics with three prong really helped me understand these skills. After I got the hang of harvesting smaller reef fish, my good friend Kiley handcrafted me my first speargun, and that was just the beginning of my spearfishing journey.

From my very first catch I was absolutely hooked on spearfishing. It's given me a new sense of appreciation for my food, ecosystem, and ability to dive. There is something so

*left* **Dropping down into underwater lava tubes with Kaila Razonable.** *right* **Selfie in work attire.**

instinctual about hunting and gathering that is deeply ingrained in us humans, and for me it is one of the most rewarding feelings. My life now revolves around ocean conditions, with diving being my number one priority. I often have underwater dreams of spearing fish, swimming with orcas, and visiting underwater mansion-sized caves. Sometimes I even waking up gasping for air.

Freediving and spearfishing are moving me around the world. Through my sense of adventure, I am able to represent Hispanic women in the outdoor space. Dancing with playful sea lions in Mexico, gliding over rainbow table corals in Fiji, and being blanketed by curious sting rays in the Bahamas are just a taste of the dreamy experiences the benevolent sea has provided. It is in these moments that I feel most alive, and most myself.

Harmony found in nature is the closest thing to perfection. The balance of millions of different variables all working together in an ecosystem is an unfathomable miracle. Living close to nature brings peace and fulfillment. Although humans are never perfect, I am motivated to live my life in ways that are sustainable and eco-friendly. Spearfishing, gardening, relying on rainwater catchment, and foraging is what this looks like to me.

One day I hope to raise children and share the wonders of the ocean with them. Imagining what the ocean might look like a few decades from now is concerning, however. Diving the Pacific over the last six years, I have noted changes caused by coral bleaching (due to warm water temperatures) that are affecting Hawai'i's beautiful reefs. Knowing that I am observing a tainted version of a healthy ocean is disheartening. Seeing the unenthusiastic efforts in conserving land and water by agencies and politicians is infuriating and depressing. In my future I hope to help spread the understanding of the ocean and environment to the next generation of watermen and women. I am inspired to give back, and will continue to be an advocate for conservation, sustainable living, and living in harmony with nature.

*left and right* **Freediving through underwater archways off of Kona, Hawai'i.**

*top* **Kicking out to the depths while scanning the reef for specific fish species to harvest.**

*bottom* **Playing in the soft white sand patches off Oahu.**

*right* **Cave running: Rock running through cathedral-like lava tubes with Lilinoe Wedemeyer on board.**

*next page left* **Spearfishing with my custom 112" roller Aimrite USA speargun, dusting in the sand to attract fish.** *top left* **Exploring the kelp forest in California. Look closely behind my head for a curious soupfin shark coming to check me out.** *top right and bottom* **Our Australian shepherd is named "Pachi," short for Menpachi, which is a delicious squirrel fish you can three prong here in Hawai'i.**

*left* **Sand patches make the best napping spot. Slowing my heart rate and relaxing allows me to hold my breath for extended periods of time.** *right* **Blowing bubble rings in the Bahamas.** *next page* **Split shot taken in a remote Bahamian grotto. Reef fish swarm these nutrient-filled waters.**

# RACHEL ROSS
# THE CANYONEER

*I wish someone had told me how simple it is for hobbies to bring you full-time joy.*

I grew up in the Midwest, forever craving experiences far beyond the comfortable. All my favorite documentaries, guidebooks, and stories were about outdoor discoveries, and all were saturated with gorgeous imagery and stunning artwork. Yet I stayed true to my inner pragmatic, receiving a geology degree from a prestigious university while juggling the idea of staying in academia for the long haul. I broke up the coursework, studying, and long hours of lab work with a new-found love of rock climbing and photography, but thought of them simply as hobbies. I wish someone had told me how simple it is for hobbies to bring you full-time joy.

After enough classroom time, hobby-enjoying, trying out various scholastic identities, and getting a degree on my wall, my future seemed like one large question mark. I looked back at college and asked myself, "What was your favorite thing you did in all those four years?" I had flashbacks to guiding freshmen through Michigan forests, or long nights at the climbing wall, drilling climbing holds into the stiff boards and watching friends climb routes I myself set. I wanted to be a guide, and I wanted to move to the desert.

The search bar was my key to the future. I typed in "west," "national park," "guiding," "jobs." The first link that came up was a canyoneering guiding job at Zion National Park, Utah, a state I had never visited, and a National Park I had maybe heard about in passing. I had never gone canyoneering in my life. But the desert sounded like a wonderful reprieve from the humid, lush forests of the Midwest. Application sent, interview done, job offered, and on a plane I went.

When you learn new skills later in life, they are usually self-taught, with adequate absorption time, practice, and—I hope—an absence of extreme consequences. When you learn to canyoneer, it's like drinking through a fire hose, with hidden technicalities that split hairs between life or death. Guiding others through it creates a whole new set of fascinating obstacles. You can read all the books, watch all the videos, and still not be prepared for the simplest of tasks in the wilderness. I fumbled through complicated knots, stretched my mental capacity while learning every variety of rescue technique for the most common hiccups—of which there are apparently quite a few—and could barely keep up with my peers during the 5 a.m. wake-up calls for formidable canyons during our off days.

What's so wonderful about the human experience is how you can at the same time be out of your element and become so invested in said element that it quickly becomes a part of you. Soon these combine together into a new identity that transforms you. That's what canyoneering did to me. I craved it, dreamed about it. And I wanted to do Heaps.

The largest canyon in the park, Heaps, was so daunting it gave me nightmares. If you look it up, you'll find mostly death and rescue reports. There's a possibility it might go overnight, the last rappel (descending via rope) is 300 feet, there are hundreds of feet of swimming, stemming (holding your body between two walls), rappelling, technical difficulties, possible obstructions with downed trees, water levels—the list goes on. But I wanted it. My best adventure pal, Cassy, trained with me my first summer. We ticked off all the intermediate and advanced

**Stemming in a Utah slot canyon is a full-body experience. You can imagine why few clothes or backpacks make it out without hefty holes.**

I went on to explore canyons that had not been touched by any human. With adoration and respect, I would take my camera through these places and feebly attempt to capture their scale and beauty.

canyons, all the while looking across the gorgeous sandstone cliffs toward our biggest objective. We assembled a crew made up of us and two other incredible adventuresses. Ropes were packed, gear devised, the plan set, and a 2 a.m. start had us on our way to completing that year's biggest goal. Four hours later, we were donning full-body wetsuits, harnesses, helmets, and other contraptions, and staring at the mouth of one of the most gorgeous canyons I've ever had the immense pleasure of experiencing. Overlapping sandstone waves guide you through the evolution of time in a way that my geology degree would never have taught me, and the stagnant pools filled with organic material reflected the orange walls, inviting me into the secret that canyons create their own environments, microclimates, and even species. About 15 seemingly endless hours later, and we were staring back up at the 300-foot rappel, safely on the ground. It was 2015, and I hadn't been aware of any other group solely made up of women who had previously completed it. I truly hope that we were not the first.

I had the honor of exploring Heaps every year since my first descent. I went on to explore canyons that had not been touched by any human, canyons that had only been touched in ways that were indiscernible to future explorers, and canyons that had been done so often that the sheltered environments were now made up of candy wrappers, footsteps, and bolts. With adoration and respect, I would take my camera through these places and feebly attempt to capture their scale and beauty. I showed very few of these photographs, and, with the rise of social media, kept even more to myself. But I did see the power of photography to change and inspire. I dragged my camera up the walls of Zion canyons, on rock climbs and hikes, and felt quite humbled by the constant fact that a simple frame could not even begin to capture the beauty in front of me.

If I could make a photo move, perhaps that would accomplish my goal. So I turned to video. I created marketing material for the guiding company I worked for, sought out people to tell stories, to capture visual stories of local happenings, and slowly improved my craft. Manipulating various modes on a video camera changes how you can affect the viewer, and the psychology behind video intrigues me to this day.

There have been a few changes since I first moved to the huge sandstone dwelling of Zion. The crowds choke the small town, the ever-moving geology leads to rock hazards that mean areas have to be closed to the public, and Cassy passed away in a canyoneering accident. I moved to the city of Salt Lake City, not

*left* **Cassy and a friend ponder life at the end of the tunnel in a central Utah canyon.** *right* **You can spot the internal structure of these walls by the curving striations and distinct layers.**

too far from the canyons, and continue to pursue cinematography. I've had the opportunity to work with names like Red Bull, Ford, and Mammut, capturing climbers, bikers, runners, and more, pursuing athletic feats that inspired little me back in the Midwest.

I call myself a cinematographer with as much pride as I have when I call myself a canyoneer, with a small asterisk. So much of my identity was wrapped up within the sandstone cliffs that I forgot the larger picture of who I could be outside of outdoor sports. Just as important as adventuring with the body is stretching the mind's capability to handle immense beauty, endurance, and the technicalities needed for long-term joy. I've found that adventuring and cinematography have a lot in common, between staying calm in the stress of it all, the physical toll it takes on your joints, and the utter joy of accomplishing long-term goals that are built upon long days in the field. I've gone from trying to encapsulate beautiful scenery in an image to capturing the emotional experiences that keep us returning to places like Heaps again and again.

*left* **Rappelling into Right Fork Canyon in Zion National Park, Utah. It was a two-day canyoneering adventure complete with pristine pools, snow bridges, and owls.**

*right* **Climbing on sharp limestone near Salt Lake City.**

*left* **A classic sport climb in the Uinta Mountains, Utah.**

*right* **"Reflected light" is when shaded walls receive light that bounces off of sunlit walls. It's the most beautiful backdrop for Shandi swimming through Pine Creek Canyon in Zion National Park, Utah.**

*left* **Keeping your hands up during a frigid swim, and after, ensures more dexterity as you navigate a technically difficult space.**
*right* **The cathedral of Pine Creek Canyon in Zion National Park, Utah.**

*top* Angels Landing, the iconic trail that leads you to gorgeous down-canyon views. *bottom left* An all-women crew descended the mysterious and infamous Kaleidoscope Canyon in Utah. *bottom right* A portrait in my natural habitat. *right* Canyonlands, Utah. Running has become a way to explore a landscape without the need for ropes. *next page* Eagle Crags in Utah after a snowstorm.

# ALICIA RIUS
# THE URBAN EXPLORER

*I wanted to feel that rush of adrenaline again, like that one time when I was a kid and tried to sneak into a neighbor's house to see their toys.*

When I tell people I take photos of abandoned places, they ask, "Why?" "Isn't it dangerous?" "Do you get scared?" "Have you encountered ghosts?" "How do you find the places, and how do you get in?" Here are the short answers: Yes, it's dangerous. Yes, I've been afraid. Yes, I've encountered a ghost. I find the places in many ways. And I go in trying not to be caught by the police.

To make a long story short, it all started with a camera. When I was a kid, my dad documented my childhood. As I was growing up, seeing my father capturing the best moments of my life led me to want to do the same. At 15 years old, I got my first point-and-shoot camera, and I took over documenting my life. In the spring of 2009, I bought my first DSLR, a second-hand Nikon D80, because I wanted to take photography more seriously. The camera didn't come with a manual, so I decided to practice as much as possible. I started shooting absolutely everything. You could even say I was annoying. Every day, with my camera, I was shooting everything I saw.

In 2010, after being fired from my job in advertising due to the global economic crisis, I was jobless for months. But one thing I did have was time. So, one cold morning in March, I went out to take photos of the snow and stumbled upon a derelict farmhouse. I went in, and the first thing I found was an old portrait from the 1950s of a kid on the day of his First Communion. The frame was half broken and the front glass was missing, but the photo was still in pretty good shape. I got goosebumps, and I couldn't understand why somebody would leave something so personal behind.

When I went home, I couldn't stop thinking about the treasures I had found. I wanted to feel that rush of adrenaline again, like that one time when I was a kid and tried to sneak into a neighbor's house to see their toys (I was caught and grounded, by the way). A few photos and some Google research later, I discovered there was a movement called "urban exploration," which involved photographing abandoned places. That day, I found my passion, and my journey as an urbex photographer started.

One of the top questions I'm asked is how I find these places. But before I get into that, I should tell you that urban exploration has three main rules: 1. You don't share the location of the house; 2. You don't break in or force an entrance; 3. You don't steal anything. So how do I find the places if people don't share their locations? The first way is to find your own abandoned place, and then trade your unique discovery for another location that somebody else has. You can find a place out of sheer luck, because somebody told you the location, or because you followed some leads (such as the architecture of the building, or a photo with a name or an address in somebody else's photos). We also follow other rules, like not posting photos of the outside, to make it more challenging to figure out the coordinates of the building.

Being true to the urbex codes of honor, I have never forced an entry. For all the houses I've photographed, I got in because there was a door open or a broken window, or after I located the owner and asked permission to go in.

**Behind the scenes inside a medieval castle. This was, for me, one of the most incredible places I've been, and I was fortunate enough to visit it three times before it was completely sacked.**

The time I was most terrified was not when I encountered a human, but what I believe was the ghost of a child.

Photographing abandoned places is no joke. Most are precarious: ceilings falling apart, holes in the floor, mold everywhere. What's worse, you never know if anyone is in there already. Being a woman visiting abandoned places puts me at a greater risk of getting hurt, robbed, or raped. So I never visit a site alone. I ask family and friends to come with me, and on occasion, I go with a complete stranger from an urbex forum (yes, super safe too …).

However, I have to say that the time I was most terrified was not when I encountered a human, but what I believe was the ghost of a child. The experience happened when I visited an abandoned tower where, according to previous renters, neighbors, and even the priest that went to purify the house, many people have heard the cry of a baby coming from one of the rooms. When my friends left the house, I was left alone in the living room, taking my last photos. Suddenly, out of the blue, I heard a loud noise as if someone had decided to throw a bunch of pans down the stairs. The house was empty, and I was alone. I felt a punch in my stomach and my heart shrank. I freaked out so much that I took my stuff and left the house without looking back. I kept saying, "I'm going now; I'm sorry, please don't manifest yourself." To this day, I still believe that what happened was supernatural, super weird, and inexplicable.

The two most challenging things for me when it comes to photographing abandoned places are accessing buildings and time management. Photographing smaller spaces is also difficult. In the case of my series of photographs taken from the back seats of abandoned cars, I had to fit myself inside a VW Beetle from the 1960s together with my tripod and camera, shrink myself so my knees wouldn't show up in the frame, avoid being caught by the landlord or the neighbors (or the police), and battle with the spiders and bees that were all over the car, all the while trying not to die from heatstroke, because those cars were like ovens in summer.

It's really hard to find abandoned places that are time capsules. Homes, mansions, castles, hospitals, nurseries, and labs that still have almost everything inside are unique. When you walk into these places, you see the table set for dinner, the cigarette on the ashtray, the bed perfectly made but covered in cobwebs. You ask yourself: What happened here? It is as if the people living or working in those places had to suddenly run away and never came back. So when I find a place that preserves almost all its contents, I get overwhelmed. I get lost with the composition, preparing the still lifes, trying new things. I can spend so much time shooting the same thing that I miss other things. Sometimes I get obsessed with an object, and I can't stop. The world disappears to me. I get so focused on what I'm doing that the rest doesn't matter. But it should, because you need to be aware of everything happening around you for your own safety. I've been reckless, to the point that once, in Belgium, in an abandoned castle, two men were stalking me, and while I was distracted, they stole my entire photography gear, my jacket, the car keys—everything but the one camera I had in my hand. It was one of the worst days of my life.

My goal with my photography is to convey the way I see the world and the way I felt while I was in these places. From one perspective, silence and dust rule there—the mystery and the unknown, the danger and the decay. But despite all the silence and the solitude, I never feel alone. These places are empty of people but full of memories and stories. I've found family albums from circa 1890, closets full of clothes from the 1940s, letters written from a husband to his wife during the Spanish Civil War. When I find these treasures, they only make sense to me if somebody else can see them. Otherwise, it is as if it never happened. Photography is my tool to connect the two worlds that I'm in: the past and the present.

Most of these forgotten places no longer exist and my photos are the only vivid memory that remains. That's why it's so important to me to immortalize these places before they disappear or fall into oblivion.

***Still waiting.* I was in Belgium when I found this incredible gem. The house had an extraordinary energy where I could feel the weight of the people who once lived here still present with me.**

*next page* ***We were waiting for you.* I remember the chills this picture gave me. The Virgin Mary, holding her son, kept following me with her eyes no matter where I positioned myself.**

ALMA MATER BONORUM STUDIORUM

*previous page top* ***She's gone.*** I barely remember photographing this one. The day before two guys robbed my camera bag with everything except the camera I was using. I suffered from a severe anxiety attack that wiped out many memories of that trip. *bottom* ***Safari.*** I found this car in the woods. Little would I've known this would be the beginning of my best-known series, "From the backseat of my car."

*right* ***The invisible castle*** was my very first time capsule. It was like traveling to the past and seeing how people from two centuries ago lived. It was spectacular.

*next page* ***Six souls.*** This nursery was the second abandoned place I found, and I was terrified because I found the belongings of a homeless person who was living on the premises. I remember shooting this scene with particular angst. The space was tiny, and I barely had room to photograph it the way I wanted. The sunshine sneaking through the mortared windows mixed with the dirty old cribs was like witnessing a battle between hope and desolation. The energy was unsettling.

# PAIGE VINCENT
# THE STORM CHASER

*The exhilaration and adrenaline I get from storm chasing is addictive and it's what keeps me coming back for more.*

You can never fully prepare for a storm. You can read weather radars, compare the prediction models to one another, and even position yourself a day early to scout the terrain, but Mother Nature is never predictable. In the days leading up to a storm I do my best to stay packed and ready to go wherever the storm will be, making sure all my equipment is charged and I have extra batteries and memory cards, because these storms are truly once-in-a-lifetime events. They will never be repeated in the exact same way, and chances are you will be the only person to get the shot you do, because each storm changes every second.

I was born and raised in a pretty conservative household in Dallas, Texas, and studied graphic design in college, but as I began to travel in my mid-twenties I was inspired by my friends in the photography field to capture these memories in a more permanent way. So when I purchased my first camera at the end of 2020, a Nikon Z50, I began documenting everything I could. I was immediately drawn to shooting landscapes, including volcanoes, lightning, and severe weather in the central plains of the United States. Over time I realized I wanted to add a unique twist to these shots, so I bought a red dress from a local thrift store and began standing in the foreground of these extreme landscapes to add a human element and scale—and the "Red Dress" series was born. While working remotely as a graphic designer, I was able to travel to places such as Guatemala, Iceland, Norway, and most of the western United States during Covid. Now I can travel more than ever, since I've moved to Colorado and am in a more central area.

I love challenging myself to photograph anything that inspires me, even if that means getting a little dirty along the way. I've always been quite the tomboy and have played sports my entire life, so hiking uphill in a dress (sometimes barefoot) is never an issue for me! As I've expanded my portfolio, I've loved using social media to collaborate with different photographers from all over the world to create a fresh perspective with the "Red Dress" series. It can be challenging at times to set up a tripod and shoot by myself, especially when the conditions are not ideal, so this has greatly increased the range of the art I can create. Until recently, there also hasn't been a huge representation of women in photography or the storm-chasing community, and I'm hoping to help change that by inspiring the younger generation of women to get involved. This past year a talented group of women started Girls Who Chase, originating here in Colorado, which has spread internationally through the help of social media. It's inspiring to see the future generations of female storm chasers being so passionate about something I've loved for years.

In Dallas, where I grew up, storms happened often and tornadoes were feared. We've all seen the movie *Twister* and that was the only reference to storms my family or I had ever encountered, so when we heard the tornado sirens go off we would immediately go to the most central location in our house—the bathroom—jump in the tub, and throw a mattress over our heads. Looking back with what I know about storms today, this was probably overkill for most of the storms that crossed our path, but it's always better to be safe than sorry.

**Standing on top of my chase vehicle to get a better view of the storm approaching.**

Time seems to stop when you're watching a tornado pass right by you.

Recently, I set off on an 11-hour journey to a storm that had great potential for a tornado and some structure, and it did not disappoint. The terrain was flat and the roads were gridded, which is a storm chaser's dream. I fueled up, set up my cameras to the best settings for the time of day, and waited. Storm chasing involves a lot of sitting and waiting, and then, when the moment is right, blasting to the ideal location to meet it. This storm in particular was a tricky one, because it had multiple targets, meaning there were two potential areas that looked good for photographing. I went with my gut and headed northeast, which paid off immensely when an EF-2 tornado dropped less than half a mile from me. Even with two cameras and how close I was, it is challenging trying to keep focus on a debris cloud of dust moving at 125mph. I always make sure I snap a few photos, but also take a moment just to take it in and appreciate what is right in front of me. Time seems to stop when you're watching a tornado pass right by you and when it's gone, the only proof you have is the photos and videos you took of it on your devices. After a few hours of reviewing photos and celebrating what an amazing natural phenomenon you've witnessed, your adrenaline finally fades and you're left exhausted, but knowing it was all worth it. In that trip I only ended up witnessing one tornado in the span of three days but in that time spent 38 hours on the road, covering 2,250 miles and visiting seven states. It was the first of many chases this 2022 chase season.

*Twister* did get some things right, however. The exhilaration and adrenaline I get from storm chasing is addictive and it's what keeps me coming back for more year after year. And the storm-chasing community is one of the most family-oriented, accepting groups of people I've ever met, who all share the same nerdy passion of chasing clouds for a brief moment of rare weather phenomena. The people that I have met in the last five years only inspire me to want to chase storms even more, and they are one of the most intelligent groups of individuals I know. I can't wait to get back out there with my family of nerds and see what this year has to offer.

*left* **A bolt strikes the ground during a mid-afternoon monsoon storm in Tucson, Arizona.** *right* **Mammatus clouds fill the sky after a storm passes through Kansas.**

*next page* **As a storm moves over the Grand Canyon, three bolts strike the canyon walls in a single moment.**

*left* **An EF-2 tornado sweeps across the Iowa plains, barely missing a barn and sending debris flying at 125mph.** *top* **With the "Red Dress" on, facing the approaching supercell near Willcox, Arizona.** *bottom* **Behind the scenes as I shoot an incoming haboob near Phoenix, Arizona.**

*top* **In-cloud lightning illuminates a storm cloud as it moves over the plains of Arizona.**

*bottom* **Paige also documents other extreme nature events such as the Fuego volcano in Guatemala.**

*right* **A mothership supercell approaches Badlands National Park in South Dakota.**

# SANDI OLUOCH
# THE CURIOUS ADVENTURER

*My goal is to show other Black people, who are often underrepresented in this type of lifestyle, that a life like this is possible if they want to pursue it.*

"Hike, dive, surf. Repeat." This is the mantra I've been telling myself as I travel the world solo. This is my story: I'm a Kenyan girl with a passion for nature, adventure, and travel doing her best to bring diversity and representation to the outdoor community and international travel. In the past three years, I've summitted two active volcanoes in Guatemala, freedived in the Philippines, swum with whale sharks in Mexico, trekked through the jungle to Machu Picchu in Peru, drunk tea in the desert with the Bedouins in Jordan, danced the night away in Colombia, eaten my way through Singapore, surfed my heart out in Costa Rica, and gone sailing in Belize. And I'm only just getting started …

I've come a long way from the girl who was once too shy to make direct eye contact with others and felt so small and insecure about the color of her skin. I was born prematurely in a hospital in Nairobi at 28 weeks old, with lungs so underdeveloped that I spent my first two weeks of life inside an incubator. A rough start, but I always joke that it shows how resilient I can be! I went on to have a pretty normal childhood and I especially loved spending time outside. I still have scars on my knees from years of playing sports, riding bikes, running, and climbing trees. There's a certain uniqueness and freedom that comes with childlike joy; it's something that I want to hold onto even as an adult.

From the beginning, my parents instilled in me a deep curiosity about the world. Along with cartoons, I watched every nature documentary on National Geographic and the Discovery Channel. I'd squeal with absolute delight when they featured Kenya. I also loved watching sports and outdoor documentaries: surfing, freediving, and travel-focused ones were some of my favorites. I remember feeling a little sad that none of them looked like me … where were the Black women? Not seeing people with skin as dark as mine in these spaces impacted my confidence and sense of self-worth. It's why I stress the importance of representation in the outdoors. It really does matter! I was a happy child, but I was unsure of myself, stumbling over my words and feeling awkward in new environments. Always feeling a little lost and incomplete.

My first taste of the person I was destined to become was when I was 15 years old and living in Tanzania. I was a freshman in high school and my school had flyers up for a trip to summit Mount Kilimanjaro. My heart skipped a beat at the thought of standing on top of the highest free-standing mountain not only on the African continent, but in the entire world. It was like auditioning for a play: Hundreds of students, including myself, went through rigorous training exercises as we did our best to prove to our teachers (who were going to lead the climb) that we were up for the challenge of a lifetime. At the end of a week full of running endless miles and swimming nonstop laps in the pool, the finalized list for the 2009 Kilimanjaro Team was posted on the bulletin board. There were 15 names and mine was one of them.

The training was intense but creative: wearing hiking boots to class in order to break them in, filling up our bags with textbooks to weight train, and weekly sunrise runs on the beach. A few months later, at almost 20,000 feet above sea level, I reached the summit of Kilimanjaro. I marveled at the world

**Valle de Cocora, Colombia. These wax palms are the tallest palm trees in the world, growing up to 200 feet tall.**

The second taste of the person I was destined to become was a solo trip to Hawai'i in an attempt to heal a broken heart.

spread out below me. I was bundled up in layers of insulated gear a few sizes too big for me, slightly delirious from the altitude, and exhausted from trudging through a blizzard all night. I might have been the happiest girl in the world that day. My first time seeing snow, and it was on top of Kilimanjaro! This was pure, unbridled adventure, and I was hooked. It was the first moment in my life when I thought: "This is exactly where I'm meant to be. This is exactly who I'm meant to be."

That same year, I took a second school trip to learn how to scuba dive in Zanzibar. As you've probably gathered at this point, my freshman year of high school was pretty epic. I went diving in some of the clearest water I had ever seen, with colorful, healthy coral reefs and abundant marine life everywhere. Again, there was the familiar feeling of purpose and euphoria. However, just like on Kilimanjaro, I found that I was the only Black girl on these trips and wished there were more Black people doing this with me. I pushed on with my course and got certified a week later. It felt so natural; I grew up by the ocean and it has always had a special place in my heart. The diving school was kind enough to Photoshop the braces out of my PADI card photo. This is something I'm very thankful for, because I still use that same photo when I visit dive centers all over the world more than a decade later.

When I was 18 years old, I moved to America. As clichéd as it sounds, moving to the US changed my life. It opened the world up to me in a way that would not have been possible otherwise, and for that I am eternally grateful to my parents for giving me the opportunity to spread my wings. Like most people in their late teens and early twenties, I was still figuring life out. I was passionate but somewhat directionless. Society says: "Go to college, get a good job, get married, buy a house, have kids." On and on it goes. I was following that trajectory but in many ways, it felt like something was missing. I was happy enough, but life was missing that extra spark I felt on top of Kilimanjaro and beneath the waves of the Indian Ocean.

After graduating college, I moved to the beautiful city of Seattle. Living in the Pacific Northwest reignited the fierce love I had for the outdoors that had lain dormant while I focused on my studies. From Monday to Friday I worked a nine-to-five job but, on the weekends, I was out hiking the trails. I felt that childlike joy creeping back into my life. While I was thrilled to be part of the outdoor community, I couldn't help but notice that I was always the only Black person. Oftentimes, I was the only person of color. It brought me back to the days of watching athletes and world travelers on TV, none of whom had skin like mine. I started to think about how the lack of diversity in the outdoor world really affected me as a child and realized that I could play a part in making sure other little Black girls could feel represented in the outdoors and around the globe. So, I bought a camera and started taking pictures of me summitting mountains and a GoPro for video footage of me diving. I used social media and photography to tell my story, and people started to take notice. I talked about race, culture, and diversity as it pertains to the outdoors and people listened.

The second taste of the person I was destined to become was a solo trip to Hawai'i in an attempt to heal a broken heart. Little did I know that heartbreak was the catalyst I needed to catapult me into the world of solo travel. I was getting on that plane and going somewhere new all by myself. What if this was a huge mistake? I questioned myself so many times, but deep down I knew it was something I needed to do. As soon as I landed and checked into my hostel, a bunch of other solo travelers in my room invited me out for a swim in the ocean. In an instant, all my worries melted away. I was barely an hour into the solo travel life, and things already felt so natural. I'll never forget swimming in the ocean under a full moon with strangers I had just met, laughing, swapping stories, and bobbing along with the calm waves. I could feel myself glowing with confidence and happiness. I hadn't felt like this in a very, very long time. I even met a boy, and he taught me how to surf for the first time. Just like hiking and diving, I felt that spark immediately, and I thought to myself: "I want to do this for the rest of my life." I came back to Seattle feeling whole again. Feeling electricity running through me.

This is my story: still unfolding and always evolving. My goal is to show other Black people, who are often underrepresented in this type of lifestyle, that a life like this is possible if they want to pursue it. To show the world that, yes, we are out here too. At the end of the day, I want to be the person 10-year-old me would have loved to see on her TV screen and in books, encouraging her to follow her dreams.

**Cordillera Blanca, Peru. Admiring the view after hiking up to Punta Union Pass at 15,617 feet on the Santa Cruz trek in Huascaran National Park. This multi-day trek takes you through the magical mountains of the Andes.**

*left* **A jeep tour across the legendary Wadi Rum desert in Jordan. Due to its otherworldly appearance, famous movies like *Star Wars* and *The Martian* were filmed here.**

*top left* **Early wake-up call to snowshoe around Mount Baker, one of Washington State's five biggest volcanoes.**

*top right* **Snoqualmie, Washington State. A quick morning snowshoe. Playing around with the powdery snow.**

*top* Palawan, Philippines. A multi-day liveaboard where we sailed from Coron to El Nido. We spent the days swimming in the water and nights sleeping on several islands along the way.

*bottom* Nairobi, Kenya. Feeding giraffes at Nairobi's Giraffe Center: a sanctuary created to protect giraffes, which are endangered species.

*right* Lamu, Kenya. Sunset cruise on a dhow boat. One of the most magical things you can do on the island of Lamu.

*left* **Hiking through fall foliage and snow at Mount Rainier National Park, Washington State.**

*top left* **Wading through the water as I make my way through the strikingly-red canyons of Wadi Mujib, Jordan.**

*top right* **Enjoying a morning stroll after camping at Lake Wenatchee, Washington State.**

# NESS KNIGHT
# THE SURVIVALIST

*I specialize in carrying everything I need to survive and thrive in some of the most hostile environments on earth, learning survival skills from tribes and walking alongside some of the most iconic wildlife.*

For more than a decade I have been an explorer and primitive survivalist, completing a diverse collection of expeditions in extreme environments all around the globe. In short, I specialize in carrying everything I need to survive and thrive in some of the most hostile and extraordinary environments on earth, learning survival skills from tribes and walking alongside some of the most iconic wildlife. The curiosity for exploration and adventure transcends culture, religion, and age, and that is what draws so many of us to it.

I am still in awe of the fact that no matter how many remote locations I tick off across the globe, it barely scratches the surface of what is still out there. People say that exploration is dead, and nowhere is uncharted anymore, but this couldn't be further from the truth. Just the other week I was racing Ed Stafford across Taiwan for his Discovery Channel show *First Man Out*, and I ended up descending rivers that no human would have set foot in for decades, centuries, if ever. I found myself river racing down boxed-in canyons with no way out. I stepped back in time to the Jurassic era, fully expecting a pterodactyl to fly out from every bend and cliff face. Not only is there ample untouched wilderness, but so too are there innumerable locations where whole regions have historically been locked into a no-man's-land due to long-term geopolitical tensions, and these are regularly opening up. Our advancements in technology mean we are able to reach previously impossible places, be that uncharted ocean floors, deep cave systems beneath the earth's surface, or the ecologically unique tops of tepuis, where weird and wonderful species have evolved in absolute isolation. Climate extremes are carving new paths through age-old ecosystems and changing what was known into something very uncertain and unpredictable. Exploration is certainly not dead.

Nor is the crucial role of wisdom from indigenous peoples across the planet. I have spent a lot of time with tribes, most recently the San Bushmen of Southern Africa, the oldest peoples on our planet, who can trace their ancestry back 200,000 years. I strongly feel that there is an urgency to bring their voices to the fore. My time with remote tribes has brought with it the realization that they are absolutely in tune with nature, acting out a symbiotic relationship with the wilderness and wildlife around them that prioritizes the continuous regeneration of the ecosystems within which they live. They understand that we are a part of nature, not separate from it. There lies within them an ability to listen to ancient instincts, tapping into an "orbital perspective," a bird's-eye view of the planet which acknowledges that if we set fire to one side of the sailboat, we all suffer and sink.

I call myself an "accidental" adventurer, as my journey to this career began unintentionally. I had taken a break from my job teaching entrepreneurship in London to stand up paddleboard over 1,000 miles (something that hadn't been done

**Upper reaches of the Essequibo River, Guyana, on a world first expedition to find and document the source of South America's third largest river. We were pushing upriver, where the jungle closed in around us, the canopy above sealed over us, and fallen trees just beneath the surface forced us out of the boats to push and heave them over the hidden obstacles. We had to be wary in the dark waters though, as enormous, toothy himara fish had a tendency to bite right through boots with fearsome sets of teeth. It didn't help that we knew caiman and pyaranas were surrounding us, though it did give a sense of urgency, which was much needed if we were to find the source anytime soon.**

*top* Descending the upper reaches of the Essequibo River, Guyana, at this point known as the Sipo River.

*bottom* En route to seek the source of the Essequibo River, Guyana, having just set up a base camp on the banks where we could no longer go any further by boat due to shallow waters. We lived off the land, which meant hunting wild boar. This backpack was made from the vines and palms of the jungle to carry the kill to where we would make our next camp that evening.

*right* At this point of the expedition, most of my day was spent in the water pushing the dugout canoes over debris below the water.

I say that I was lucky, but the truth is that we create luck by actively looking for the open doors to wedge a foot into.

before at that time) down an iconic river, and never returned home. Being the opportunist that I am, I jumped on the realization that people wanted to live vicariously through my storytelling, which was thriving thanks to the advent of social media. I was lucky enough to ride the crest of this wave, and able to quickly spot the possibility to turn a passion for exploration into a full-time career.

I say that I was lucky, but the truth is that we create luck by actively looking for the open doors to wedge a foot into. Never stop visualizing where you want to go in life, because the fact is that we only see the things we are looking for; the rest fades into our peripheral vision. Make sure you are not spending your days consumed by your fears, but rather note them, give them their space, and then graft daily to pull the dreams and goals you want to see happen to the forefront of your focus. Suddenly a kaleidoscope of possibilities will spring forth from the shadows, and new paths will reveal themselves.

In April 2018 I successfully completed a world-first "source to sea" descent of the Essequibo River in Guyana, the third largest river in South America. Our expedition was everything we hoped it would be, with a fair few more close calls than we would have liked. There is nothing like waking up in the middle of the night to a jaguar tail brushing the bottom of your hammock to make you feel alive. Our 4 a.m. alarm clock was the guttural roars of howler monkeys thundering across the jungle canopy, raising the hairs on the back of my neck. The fact that emergency evacuation is impossible (with no one providing winch access on a helicopter, we were told we would have to cut down an area of primary rainforest approximately the size of a football pitch for a landing pad, which was not in the realms of doable) made close calls—like the day my colleague Pip ended up with her buttocks one inch away from a defensive pit viper ready to strike—all the more heart-stopping. That would have been curtains for her. I was suspected of having dengue fever, many got malaria, infections threatened to put an end to our expedition, and foot rot meant one member of our team was walking around with hundreds of tiny craters in her foot, looking like a ninety-something-year-old, and barely able to move from crippling pain. Navigating rapids in uncharted territory where no human had set foot before was humbling. We had no way of knowing what to expect, even with old satellite imagery, as we were traversing these lands in dry season and the river was unrecognizable compared to what had been captured from space a decade before. We found ourselves going down far too many raging rapids backwards and realized that this would be a baptism of fire like no other, even for the enormously experienced Wai Wai warriors who had grown up alongside wild river waters. But these are all the ingredients of a real-life expedition filled with peril and success in equal measure.

The expedition aimed to redefine modern exploration, putting to one side the old days of chest beating and flag planting, as the team pulled together an incredible international collaboration with the indigenous Wai Wai tribe to locate the river's source, something that had never before been found or documented. This expedition gave the Wai Wai, a marginalized people within their own country, the opportunity to use our media engine and exposure to showcase their extraordinary knowledge and affinity with the pristine primary rainforest that

**Training for the Essequibo expedition had to be done during the winter months in the UK. Some of our greatest and toughest river portages and descents were in the heart of Wales, battling to use our numb limbs that were frozen and by now felt wooden. It was a far cry from the excruciating heat and humidity we would be facing in the jungle, but nevertheless, it helped us build the fortitude and doggedness we would need when pushed to our limits for months on end.**

NRS
NRS
NRS

orca
orca

Fear is good. It keeps you attentive to what is happening around you. This is a crucial part of our evolution and survival as a species.

they call their backyard, and ultimately become guardians for the conservation of that region.

I was never particularly good at sports. I am totally uncoordinated, with little spatial awareness (walking into door frames is not an unusual occurrence). I was also an extremely shy, introverted kid at school. So, what gives me the right to become an explorer and endurance adventurer? It comes down to how I choose to define myself. For years I defined myself as that ungainly kid I just described. But the second I changed that vision and defined myself as a person who dared greatly—who relentlessly sought out courageous endeavors—something weird happened. I took on the mindset of that kind of a person and it all became real. Visualization and how you choose to define yourself is so powerful.

You don't just wake up one day and suddenly become happy, confident, entrepreneurial, or courageous. It is a practice you have to keep up, make a habit, and form routines for. You have to keep working on your internal dialogue, and consciously take control of, and responsibility for, your thoughts and emotions on a daily basis. There aren't innately confident people and weak people; there are people who actively make it happen day by day and those who do not. It is a choice, not a gift that only a few are lucky enough to be born with.

One thing expeditions teach you very quickly is the difference between fear and panic, and why this is so important. Fear is good. It keeps you responsive and attentive to what is happening around you. Potential threats are forefronted for assessment and we stay in a high alert state. This is all healthy and a crucial part of our evolution and survival as a species. Panic, however, is dangerous. It is an uncontrolled response to fear when you have lost the ability to hold your composure, and poor decisions are more often than not the outcome. Drifting from a fear state (alert yet still problem solving) into a panic state—from my personal experience—usually involves me letting my imagination go unchecked, allowing it to spew forth a tsunami of despairing outcomes that totally overwhelm me. Studies have shown that our brain struggles to tell the difference between a real event and one imagined so vividly it feels real. Our bodies respond to both real and imagined events in much the same way, increasing heart rate and stress levels if those events are negative. That's why endurance athletes and Olympic athletes spend so much time visualizing and mentally rehearsing their winning run, swim, cycle, throw, or jump. They know all too well that they can make or break the performance of their lives simply with their thought patterns. We are masters at creating highly emotional responses within ourselves from our thoughts alone.

I often get asked why I do what I do. I love exploration because it brings me a balance of the harsh realities our planet is facing, and a powerful hope that stems from the incredible people I meet and the truly wild places I traverse through. The fact is that we have all the tools and technology to be able to solve the problems we face today. What we need are the minds and hearts of people willing to be a part of that change. If we continue business as usual, we are in real trouble. We are currently running at a rate of extinction that is 1,000 times the natural rate—nature simply cannot adapt fast enough to the staggering speed of change from human impact. Filming, writing, and speaking about these journeys in far-flung corners of our planet gives me an opportunity to effect change, and bring meaningful stories from around the globe into people's living rooms and hearts.

I have an innate need to live life a little on the edge, seeking out raw, unique experiences. Importantly, though, I now have more of a sense of self and of achievement from looking back at the courage I was able to summon to face some of the scariest moments of my life, than I do from whether or not I achieved my goals. I am proud of my failures because I had the courage to get back up. They mean more in the end than the momentary highs of successes, because they took real grit.

**Training in London just prior to becoming the first female in history to swim the length of the Thames River from its source.**

Billboard H4

*left top* **Exploring the raw and rugged little-known corners of Scotland, accessing wild camping island spots that were not accessible by any other means.**

*left bottom* **Assessing rapid systems to choose the best line before descending with the team in uncharted jungle regions of the Essequibo River, Guyana.**

*top* **The final day of a world first, crossing the most remote regions of Namibia by fat bike. The finale was a tough slog through the world's oldest desert, the Namib.**

*bottom* **Machete at the ready as we hacked through the tangle of vines and fallen trees that blocked our way upstream on the Essequibo River, Guyana.**

*previous page* **A brief moment of respite while on the frontlines of the war on poaching, tracking rhino on foot in southern Africa during the filming of an investigative documentary following the illicit international trade of rhino horn.**

*top* **Filming up close and personal with rhino in the Western Cape, South Africa. The security on reserves that home wild rhino comes at a cost of millions due to the poaching epidemic. Rhino are currently worth more dead than alive due to poaching carried out by criminal syndicates that feed demand coming from East Asia.**

*bottom* **Spending a month with the San Bushmen in Namibia, learning primitive survival skills from a people who have been around for 200,000 years. This image captures the stages of making my bush clothing from hide, tanning wild animal skins.**

*right* **At home on my farm in Yorkshire, UK, with an orphan lamb. We work our homestead to be as self-sufficient as possible, growing and raising all of our own food.**

# SHALEE WANDERS
# THE ADVENTURE TRAVELER

*I'm acutely aware of my surroundings and grateful to be everywhere I end up.*

I've always been an overambitious dreamer. Sometimes I think my excessive optimism has led me down the path of becoming an adventure writer, photographer, and explorer. However, I'm not sure I'll ever be used to it. I'm acutely aware of my surroundings and grateful to be everywhere I end up.

But it wasn't always like that. A decade ago, I was 18, attempting to escape from my tiny rural hometown in Michigan. Back then, I spent most of my weekends visiting my mother in jails and rehabs around the state with my brother and father. My dad was working the nighttime custodial shift at our local high school, doing the best he could to support our family. I spent most nights alone, wondering what life would be like after losing our house. The day the bank took over, the last thing that hung on the walls of my lime-green bedroom was a bucket list that stretched from the ceiling to the floor. I distinctly remember sitting on the stained carpet, staring up at the list, and crying. Oh, how far away those dreams seemed. The following summer I lived with my grandparents and worked at a local ice cream shop. I was making $6 an hour and irresponsibly spent most of it on gas money to drive to the Great Lakes, sleeping in my car, camping to save money, and watching sunsets whenever possible. It wasn't much, but I felt like I was exploring for the first time in my life.

Growing up with a mother who was battling addiction made me inherently aware of our mortality. At first, it battered me with anxiety that hindered any attempt to leave. I was afraid of a lot of things in the world, afraid of what could happen if I left. I let that define me for far too long. But eventually, the anxiety motivated me in a very different way. I had stared death in the face many times. We are all going to die. We never know when and we won't always know how, but it will happen to every single one of us. And no matter what you believe happens to us after death, we might as well have the most fun possible at this moment.

I realized this when my life changed. At the time I was wrapping up my final year at community college, where I worked as a support staff member on campus. I began spending my weekends driving around to every corner of the Midwest. One of the first moments I truly felt alive was on a weekend camping trip in Tobermory, Canada, when I decided to do a 75-foot cliff jump into the waters of Lake Huron. Looking back, it was not one of my smartest moves and not something I would necessarily recommend. But it was one of my first big risks, and I felt a rush and a love of life.

Immediately after graduation from Michigan State University two years later, I turned down a full-time job offer to jet off to Europe for three months with my boyfriend (now husband). We had each saved $10,000 working multiple jobs and decided to see how long we could travel on it. There are a lot of people who backpack in Europe, but our methods were quite unconventional. A week or so into the adventure, we realized we were spending very little money and decided to see if we could manage $20 per person per day for three months. We tracked every expense, from thirty-cent coffees to overpriced chocolates in Switzerland. Because we had no itinerary and it was Europe in peak summer, we spent most nights wild camping, sometimes illegally when we got stranded or unexpectedly kicked off trains because our Eurail pass didn't cover the route. We even spent a night under a bridge in Spain, one night in a drainage tunnel in Italy, a few nights in

**Sunset in Canyonlands National Park during a road trip through Utah.**

There are far too many people in this world who live in their comfort zone and fail to ever follow their dreams.

ditches, and one very long night in Eastern Europe taking turns napping on the street while people waited nearby for us to doze off so they could rob us. We got stuck in Bulgaria after we were unable to cross into Turkey due to the coup attempt and decided to climb the tallest mountain in Greece on a whim after a train strike left us stranded for three days in the town of Litochoro.

During this time, we walked an average of 10 miles a day, only riding in a car when we could hitch. Our stove stopped working halfway through the trip and we ate cold canned beans and naan bread as a meal more than once. One day in Norway, we decided to hop off the train in a remote area with only a rail station and hike into the wilderness to see what we could find. Many miles later, we came upon a remote lake and a perplexed group of Norwegian fishermen, who were wondering how a pair of Americans ended up out here roaming the tundra with the musk oxen and reindeer. As odd as it sounds, we felt more comfortable there than in any city in Europe. We had no home, but oddly, anywhere in the backcountry felt like it.

It was here that I gained my unofficial title of "backcountry bathroom expert." The end tally for the 90-day trip came to $3,440 each. This included our round-trip plane tickets, $1,100 each for an unlimited three-month Eurail train pass, food, clothing, and accommodation. We spent so little we decided to buy a rusted-out 2001 GMC Savanna for $1,900 when we got back to travel the States for the next seven months. During that time, our backcountry adventures began elevating, as we searched for high points and remote summits to score on the road. Eventually, we began attempting our modified version of the 50 State Highpointing Club, a group dedicated to summitting the tallest point in every state. Our version meant that we were attempting every state with a high point over 5,000 feet, eliminating most high points outside of the east coast except for a handful in the Appalachian Mountains.

I'm now 28 and wish every day that I could go back in time and tell 18-year-old Shalee that the next 10 years would include nearly 40 countries, 49 states, and adventures that would take her to some of the most remote mountains and wilderness across the world. That she took the leap, followed her dreams, and now lives at the base of the Rocky Mountains in her favorite town of Cody, Wyoming. All that stuff is pretty cool, but to be honest I think younger me would be most excited about the fact that we now have two adventure cats road-tripping and climbing things with us.

In 2017, we fostered five cats (one mom, four kittens), and in the end were left staring down at two furry faces we couldn't give up. They were so small, so fragile, and so full of wonder about the world. We weren't sure how they would alter our adventures moving forward, but we knew that we weren't letting them go.

To our surprise, those eight-week-old kittens took to the road with courage and force, sitting on our laps and staring out the window at the countryside passing by as we traveled. We began taking them on daily walks when they were five months old. Now, they climb, camp, and hike around the country with us, no leashes or crates necessary. Many people believe cats can't travel or hike because we are conditioned to think they can't. But they make fantastic travel partners if you work with them early and train them consistently.

What I want this story to share is that life is never going to provide the perfect moment to alter your destiny. My motto has always been that I would rather say "oh well" than "what if." That one phrase has defined who I am today. I work remotely from some of the most scenic locations around the country. I get to inspire others and bring them on worldwide adventures. I still have never paid more than $650 for an international plane ticket. I spend my weekends laying in fields of wildflowers under towering granite spires. I know, it still feels unreal to me, too.

*top* **Scrambling, hiking, and playing in the mud throughout numerous slot canyons after days of unseasonally heavy rainfall in southern Utah.**

*bottom left* **Sitting beneath Mount Whitney, California, the tallest point in the continental 48 states, where Josh and I got engaged after a successful summit via the Mountaineer's Route in 2019.**

*bottom right* **Our adventure cat, Maverick, exploring sand dunes in eastern Idaho.**

Thinking back to those days along Lake Michigan, I remember a specific night when the water was so calm you couldn't tell where the ripples met the sky. I stared at it for a long while, questioning whether what others thought of me was true. If I was crazy, a dreamer, an oddball. And now I want everyone to know that I take those words as an absolute compliment. There are far too many people in this world who go by the book, live in their comfort zone, and fail to ever follow their dreams. They've never felt the rush of running into the ocean at midnight. They definitely don't have a journal of their most scenic bathroom breaks. And they'll probably never know what it's like to scream at the top of their lungs from the summit of a mountain.

What defines your adventure is uniquely your own. I will never climb the tallest mountain in the world. I will probably never hold any sort of record. But I will continue to enjoy each and every adventure I take, no matter how big or how small it seems.

*previous page left* **In a local whiskey store in rural Scotland, I noticed a shipwreck picture hanging in a rusted old frame. With little knowledge of the area, I scouted Google Maps until finding evidence of a shipwreck on a nearby beach.** *previous page right, top left* **Maverick on his daily walk in our home of Cody, Wyoming.** *previous page right, top right* **A break along a 17-mile hiking day in America's southwest.** *previous page right, bottom* **When researching an upcoming trip to Italy, I found a Google Maps pin of a mountain hut located high above Lake Como. At that moment I knew I had to trek to the clouds to find it.**

*right* **A moment of pure joy and excitement after shooting one of my favorite sunsets in Canyonlands National Park, Utah.**

*top* **Camping in the middle of snowfields during a backpacking trip on the border of Montana and Wyoming.** *right* **Soaking up summer in Grand Teton National Park, the day before making a summit attempt on Teewinot Mountain, Wyoming.**

*previous page left* **The entrance to a hidden cave in Idaho.** *previous page right* **On one of many mountain adventures in the Absaroka Mountain Range in Wyoming with our other adventure cat, Aspen.** *left* **High in the Italian Alps after finding a $500 round-trip plane ticket from Wyoming to Milan.** *top* **On a road trip along the Great Ocean Road in southern Australia.**

# LUCY SHEPHERD
# THE EXPEDITION LEADER

*When we think of an explorer, an image of a 19th-century male figure with a big beard and woolly hat is very likely to come to mind, or maybe—and inevitably—we think of Indiana Jones.*

One of the first things that strangers like to ask is, "What do you do?" I used to feel a tad awkward when answering this question with no context, but now I try my hardest to reply unapologetically and with pride. "I'm an explorer," I say. I am very aware this sounds ridiculous, and it is often followed by a response of "Sorry, a what?"

Don't get me wrong, I didn't grow up thinking that to be an explorer or an adventurer was a real job. Hey, I didn't even think explorers still existed in our modern world. Let's be honest, when we think of an explorer, an image of a 19th-century or Edwardian male figure with a big beard and woolly hat is very likely to come to mind, or maybe—and inevitably—we think of Indiana Jones. I certainly don't look like either of those: I'm a 29-year-old blonde female. However, isn't it about time we changed that image and redefined what an explorer is and who they can be? Being an explorer is about experiencing somewhere new and unfamiliar for the very first time, and that is exactly what I have found a career in doing.

I have been leading expeditions for over a decade. I was lucky enough to join a 10-person team in the Arctic of Svalbard for 10 weeks when I was just 18 years old. It shaped me into the person I am today. During that expedition I realized my potential and was introduced to a version of myself whom I loved and admired. It was there that I found a deep connection to extreme wilderness environments and found that I felt a duty to protect them. Ever since, I have considered it my responsibility to foster this sense of awe as widely as possible, connecting others to the Earth as stewards, not spectators. Returning to normality after that first expedition was never an option. Yet, as I shared my realization with those around me, it seemed apparent to them (and abhorrent to me) that, since such an expedition was "once in a lifetime," I'd never see or feel the world like that again. From that moment I knew that I wanted a lifetime of adventure. I needed to experience everything in the furthest-flung corners of this planet and share my experiences with others to inspire a larger connection to our world.

Adventure has become my oxygen over the years and I am the first to admit that I am not the same person without it. Now that it is also my profession, it's no longer an escape but my daily life. Adventure has been the catalyst to seeing who I really am and I feel privileged to have that insight, as it's one that surprisingly few get to experience.

The magic of expeditions is that they catapult us into a primal existence. Every decision is important and in order to survive and thrive, you have to stay alert, focus, and live in the present. Adventure shows us how strong we can be even in the darkest of times, because there is simply no other choice. I really do believe that we all have this strength within us; it's just about harnessing and discovering it. Adventure can provide an opportunity for just that.

Over the years, I've found myself in the deep, untouched, and uncharted Amazon rainforest, at the tops of the highest mountains, and swimming from iceberg to iceberg in the high Arctic. The nature of my work has meant that I've got close to

**Descending a 23,000 foot peak in the Pamir mountains, Tajikistan. Tensions were high when this photograph was taken as it felt like the mountain was crumbling beneath our feet. We'd had a night of consistent rock fall and avalanches in the surrounding area and we just wanted to get back to safety.**

I have great respect for what my body and mind have gone through when the elements have been against me.

the edge and looked death directly in the eye on a number of occasions, but one thing's for certain: I don't have a death wish. This isn't about adrenaline-fueled adventure or seeing just how far I can push it, it's about maximizing life's potential, calculating every risk in order to feel fulfilled. It isn't about death, it's about living.

"Bravery" is a term often used to describe adventurers and explorers, but bravery is not about taking physical risks; instead it's about taking on something where there is a possibility that you might fail. My journey toward becoming an explorer has been anything but easy. There was no guidebook or checklist to follow and no guarantee that I would get here. I've faced hurdle after hurdle along the way. One of those hurdles, unsurprisingly, is the preconceptions others have of me, resulting in imposter syndrome on my end. Those preconceived ideas of others are still in the shadows, but thankfully, I have my own ways of dealing with them.

My experiences have allowed me to grow into someone I'm proud of. I have great respect for what my body and mind have gone through when the elements have been against me. Our complex and hectic 21st-century lives can be overwhelming at times and it can be empowering to think back to how I have harnessed self-belief, courage, and grit and draw strength from my past self.

One of the biggest takeaways I have had from these expeditions is just how much every single one of us needs to be in nature. There has not been a single person that I've been with on an expedition who hasn't benefited in some way from being in the outdoors. Everyone is more open; there are no barriers, no walls put up. Humans find peace in the natural world and are happier for it, and it wouldn't do us any harm to recognize that.

Like a lot of explorers, I am an optimist. I am optimistic for our future just as I am optimistic when beginning an expedition. The appetite for adventure is increasing and in turn, so is our desire to protect this paradise in which we live. In this brutal yet beautifully paradoxical world, only one thing's for sure: The best is always yet to come.

*left* **Pulling a pulk (sled) across the Arctic Finnsmarkvidda during a crossing of the plateau in Norway.** *right* **Reaching the summit of a peak during a ski-mountaineering crossing of the High Sierras. It had been touch and go whether we'd make it safely up this face due to the unstable conditions but thankfully we made it up just before the sun had time to bake it.**

*top* **Standing on the snowy mountain ridge whilst climbing the infamous Mount Denali, Alaska.**

*left* **Warming up in the morning Arctic sunrays.**

*right top* **Catching food with a bow and arrow is an important skill to have when moving in the jungle for months on end.**

*right bottom* **There's no better feeling than completing an expedition successfully. This is the moment where we emerged from the deep jungle after 50 days going through uncharted territory.**

# JILL HEINERTH
# THE CAVE DIVER

*Most people look into the darkness of a cave and see only terrifying blackness. I see an unexplored world of possibilities.*

As a cave diving explorer, I swim through the veins of Mother Earth, immersed in the lifeblood of our planet. Most people look into the darkness of a cave and see only terrifying blackness, but for me, the darkness beckons, drawing me into an unexplored world of possibilities. Every fin stroke that takes me further into the unknown offers an opportunity for discovery and growth.

Cave diving has been characterized as the world's most dangerous sport and the edgy frontier of earthbound scientific exploration. In this extreme form of technical diving, aquanauts pierce through the veil of permanent darkness, swimming through a maze of subterranean limestone landscapes all over the globe. Dedicated enthusiasts, adventurous researchers, and scientists race to explore the perilous conduits, deploying multiple scuba tanks, high-tech rebreathers, and underwater scooters capable of breakneck speeds, achieving penetrations logged in miles rather than feet.

To a filmmaker and photographer, underwater caves represent the ultimate challenge: I create art while monitoring delicate life support equipment at task loads that take my mind and body to the limit. Despite the risk, I'm like a kid in a candy store, working with biologists discovering new species, physicists tracking climate change, and hydrogeologists examining our finite freshwater reserves. Probing the underground pathways of the planet, I've found grisly sources of pollution, the roots of life inside Antarctic icebergs, and the ancient skeletal remains of Mayan civilizations sacrificed in the cenotes of the Yucatan peninsula. It is a privilege to uncover these hidden shrines and share concealed mysteries found deep inside our planet.

Today, we live in a world where fear influences the actions of the populace. People are terrified of world events, failure, and change in their daily lives. If we allow fear to govern our existence, then there is only one outcome: the status quo. The secret to growth is finding a way to swim into the unknown instead of sinking into reactionary oblivion. I am not suggesting that you cast away fear and run headlong into danger. It is more important to embrace a certain amount of fear in your life, enough to stimulate growth.

People often suggest that I might not want to dive with them because they are afraid. My response is, "You are precisely the type of person that I wish to dive with." Being fearful means that you care about the outcome of your endeavors. Fear helps you make good choices about risk versus reward. Fear drives you to move closer to the edge and take on things that inspire growth. When we work to liberate ourselves from the restraints of fear, then personal limitations expand. We can develop our potential.

Fear resides in humanity as a defense mechanism. Our primal instincts are programmed-in responses intended to keep us alive. That preconditioning may keep us safe from harm but is not necessarily designed to increase our potential. When we find ourselves in danger, our bodies respond with fight or flight. However, I would suggest another option. In the face of danger, it can be overwhelming to envision success or survival. It is all too easy to lash out or run screaming for the closest source of comfort. But in my job, either of those options can end in death. When trapped in a claustrophobic cave underwater in the darkness of a total silt-out, I must summon the calmness

**In a cave called "The Pit" in Mexico's Yucatan, the sunbeams stream into the depths, illuminating a diver.**

Be willing to assume risk. Be bold and confident in whatever you take on in life.

*left* **I lived near Florida's Ginnie Springs for more than a decade, making hundreds of dives into the caves onsite.**

*right* **Peering into an unusual waterhole in a hypersaline lake in Egypt.**

necessary to make the next best step towards survival. If a rock has me pinned, I use logic to figure out how to free myself. If the safety guideline breaks, I methodically deploy my cave diver's reel and patch the broken guideline. I must do all of these things in the absence of panic. Every breath I take has to be measured and calm. I must keep my heart rate low and focus on the next best course of action. Unchecked emotions won't serve me in this life-threatening situation. They will only distract me from success and use up precious air. Pragmatism and confidence must rule the moment so that I can solve my dilemma and get back out of the cave.

Whether you are a salesperson trying to figure out how to reach a quarterly target or a researcher looking for a cure for a disease, it can be overwhelming to find a way to envision solutions to big problems. It can be hard to know what success might look like or when it will come. But I challenge readers to consider the simple fact that we are all capable of making the next best decision at crucial moments of our lives. In the depths of our subconscious, we know what we should do next. And if we keep making positive steps toward our most meaningful goals, we will achieve great things.

How can you apply this? When fear gets in the way, ask yourself, "If I take this risk and take responsibility for my choice, what might be the rewards? What is the worst thing that could happen?" By taking responsibility, you choose your destiny. By moving methodically toward a solution, you can overcome almost any roadblock.

People look at my work and suggest that documenting the world of underwater caves might be the most dangerous job in existence. I have been burdened with the grief of countless colleagues' deaths, some of whom made unwise choices in the blackness of underwater cave systems. Their names have been added to a long list of divers who ran out of air, got lost in a labyrinth, or pressed too far into new exploration before turning back. With training, preparation, and dedication to proper safety procedures, I have maintained a career of nearly 30 years of exploration and science. It would be arrogant to say that I will never make a mistake or poor choice that could ultimately cost me my life, but I believe that following the ultimate rule for survivors can help. Be willing to assume risk. Be ready to push the razor's edge of possibility. Be bold and confident in whatever you take on in life. Embrace the fear of the unknown and bring it into your decision-making at every step. But finally, when you are within sight of success, within arm's reach of grasping the treasure you seek, you must still listen to that intuition. When the hair stands up on your neck, alerting you to danger ahead, you must be willing to let go. As you reach for the tempting summit of the mountain or the new exploration in a virgin cave, remember you also have to get home safely. Knowing when to turn back is as essential as embracing fear in the first place. Patient, diligent work is the key to an explorer's success. Swim boldly into new endeavors with the knowledge that you may not achieve your ultimate goal the first time around. Take a deep breath, focus, and make the next best choice.

*right* **A cave in Abaco, Bahamas.**

*next page left* **Slipping through a restriction called "The Lips" wearing a special life support device called a rebreather.** *right top* **A breath of fresh air after a long cave dive.** *right bottom* **A diver squeezes through a narrow bedding plane at Ichetucknee Springs in Florida.**

HOLLIS

# CARME FONTANET
# THE NEXT-LEVEL SOLO TRAVELER

*After following blindly what society prescribed to me as well as to all my peers, a feeling of deep emptiness started crippling me.*

My story starts like most stories, but let me put you in context. I grew up in a small town in the northeast of Spain, near Barcelona, but less cool than the birthplace of the Sagrada Familia and Barça Football Club. When I turned 18, I moved to Barcelona to go to college. Living and working as a graphic designer in the big capital city was all I had dreamed about since I was a teenager. My college time passed and a couple of years later, I was finally living my dream life. But here is where the real story begins.

After following blindly what society prescribed to me as well as to all my peers, a feeling of deep emptiness started crippling me. I felt that it was like a spider following me wherever I went, and I ended up naming that spider "depression." As time went by, I kept feeding the spider with the sadness I was feeling without even realizing it, and so the spider was getting bigger and bigger until it got to the point where I couldn't carry it any longer. I had hardly any energy left, and it was difficult to feel any motivation at all, but I knew I had to make a move and ditch the spider for good if I wanted to give life another chance. At that point, the only strong emotion I could really feel was fear. And so, I took the decision to face my fear of traveling alone. At 23 years old, I left my apartment, quit my job, said goodbye to all my friends and family, and bought a one-way ticket to India. Let me tell you, it wasn't as fun as it can look on Instagram, but the day I was standing alone in the airport, surrounded by strangers from all over the world, I felt the most fearful and the most alive I had felt in a long time.

Why did I choose India as my first destination? Well, as I told you, I needed some fear to get me out of bed, but that being said, I wouldn't recommend that anyone goes to India for the first time alone. Why? Because I went from the lowest hygiene standard I've ever experienced to seeing the sickest and poorest people my eyes had ever seen until that point, and I was even sexually harassed. But, as paradoxical as it may sound, it was exactly all those hard situations which made me aware of how lucky I am to have the option to go back to my own country, where things are very different. It made me realize how fortunate I am, but also how ungrateful I had been in the past, taking all the abundance we have as Westerners for granted. All the hardships and struggles I experienced in India meant a shift on my perspective in life, and that was a big game-changer for me.

Following my fears has been a huge blessing, because it taught me how limitless I am. With experience, I discovered that behind fear there's always something greater than yourself, a letting go of all the memories who defined the old you. Behind fear, there's always an expansion of the idea of who you are now versus the person you thought you were before. Of course, this mindset shift didn't happen in just one day. It took some tears, a few "What the fuck am I doing with my life?" moments, and a lot of almost quitting. But I had to grow up from the old me to the new me. I had to learn to be by myself because I was the only one I could rely on to keep me safe. I was the only one who could take care of myself. I simply had to fall in love with myself again, so I could explore and redefine the limits of my fears.

Traveling alone for the first time to India was a bigger deal than it might sound. I went from sitting at the same desk in front

**Cairo, Egypt. I was doing a photoshoot with a friend on the street, and everyone was staring at us.**

گسترش میدان مقاومت

I went through one of the hardest yet most powerful experiences I've ever had, a Vipassana retreat.

of a computer for eight hours a day to walking down the ghats in Varanasi, India, with a sadhu who drank from a human skull. After two hard months in India and experiencing the craziest adventures, I kept traveling around Central Asia and Southeast Asia. I was lucky enough to visit Indonesia, where I lived for two months with a French family in their dreamy villa on the beautiful island of Bali. In Thailand, I went through one of the hardest yet most powerful experiences I've ever had, a Vipassana retreat. This 10-day silent meditation retreat changed my life forever as I got more in touch with my inner self, and it's no surprise that since that experience I have kept practicing meditation to this day. From Thailand, I went to Laos, where I spontaneously decided to buy a manual motorbike and drive it all the way up to the northern border with Vietnam and cross both countries from west to east. Later I decided to sell my fabulous but crusty Honda 120 and head up by bus to Cambodia, where I started working as a yoga teacher for the first time. It was then that I felt called to go back to India, and that's exactly what I did. I gave India another chance, and so I ended up spending three months in the country, but this time in the south, where I took a break from traveling and started taking meditation and yoga more seriously. I even took classes in Indian philosophy. This time I really fell in love with the country that I'd once hated. My last destination before Covid-19 turned the world upside down was Sri Lanka, where I lived for three months, surfing, teaching yoga, meditating, and enjoying life. But everything has to end, and so it did.

Covid came, and it meant a big change in my life again. Going back to my hometown after more than a year of living in seven different countries with just one small backpack was just as crazy as all the other adventures, or maybe even more so. I guess it's not the type of adventure anyone would seek. Honestly, I feel like I handled the first weeks pretty well, but after a while I started again to pursue the conventional lifestyle my naive teen self had once dreamed about. For some reason, I was starting to think about my 15 months of backpacking experience as just a phase, but thankfully, it didn't take me too long to realize what was crystal clear. Sitting all day in front of a computer was killing the spark which kept me feeling alive through all my travels. Being back living paycheck to paycheck and knowing exactly how my weeks and months were going to look was killing all the excitement. In this developed world there was no space for

*left* **Bazaar of Tabriz, Iran. In these kinds of places, you can only see men reading newspapers while smoking shisha and drinking tea because women are not allowed.** *right* **Visiting the beautiful mosques in Shiraz, Iran.**

> As I already had some experience traveling alone, I decided to take my journey to the next level and explore by myself the areas considered dangerous and unsafe, especially for women.

surprises, or mystery. No space to enjoy the unknown. Everything was planned months and months ahead.

It was clear: This life is not fun. This life is not for me. The month of November came and with it a big decision: I would again conquer my fear of traveling solo. And so, I grabbed my old and dusty backpack from the closet and took it with me on a plane far away from my comfort zone. This time I wasn't dropped off in the middle of green lush tropical jungles in Asia, but in the hot deserts of the Middle East.

As I already had some experience traveling alone, I decided to take my journey to the next level and explore by myself the areas of the world which are considered the most dangerous and unsafe, especially for women. It was time to swap monkeys for camels, and monsoon rain for 115-degree heat. I decided once more to buy a one-way ticket, but this time to explore Egypt, the country of pharaohs. And of course, if one seeks the unexpected, the unexpected ends up happening. After visiting countries such as Egypt, Turkey, Israel, Palestine, and Iran, I fell in love with the culture and the people of the Middle East. I wouldn't be honest with you if I told you these countries are easy to travel in, but everywhere I go I face some challenges. As I keep overcoming my fears, I feel a stronger connection with myself, which allows me to move forward and overcome all the obstacles and hard times with more ease than before. And let me tell you, I'm no braver than anyone else—I have the same fears as all other humans, if not more—but I choose to be friends with the fear instead of running away from it. To see how far I've come is worth every challenge I go through, and that's exactly what keeps me seeking new adventures and new countries, where I might have to face very different and not so pleasant realities, like having to wear a hijab and cover my whole body as I did in Iran.

When I come back to my hometown now, I don't fall back into the idea of fitting in and pursuing the dreams of others. Now, when I decide to come back to Spain, I feel blessed to have peace in my country, I feel blessed to be able to wear shorts and tank tops whenever I want, blessed to have a safe place I can call home, and so much more. I stopped taking things for granted long ago. Although it's not easy to keep this mindset when everyone around you is complaining about everything, I ground myself every day with the thought that I must keep consciously choosing what I want to do with the most precious thing we have—time.

I made myself a promise to not follow the comfort everyone worries about in our society, but instead to chase my fears as I keep traveling alone to the most unpopular countries to expand my limits and to choose to live fully on my own terms. After all my adventures around more than 15 countries outside Europe, I can say firmly that traveling to the unknown is what makes me feel the most alive. That's why I put all my time and energy into my work as a full-time traveler, so I can share the cultures I get to know as a solo female traveler, and my not-so-common lifestyle and experiences, with the rest of the globe.

*top* **Beautiful scene shot in the Taj Mahal, India.**

*bottom left* **The Old Bazaar of Cairo, Egypt.**

*bottom right* **Lleida, Spain.**

*top* **Me and my Egyptian friend visiting his friend's shop in the city of Luxor, Egypt. His friend gifted me a full bag of delicious peanuts.**

*left and right* **Visiting a local bakery in Rasht, Iran, where they cook a very special bread called sangak.**

*left* **Beautiful scene at the Taj Mahal, India.**

*top left* **This Indian family came to me when I was visiting their town in the Desert of Jaisalmer.**

*top right* **Taking the bus in Tabriz, Iran, where there is an area only for women. Men and women travel separately.**

*next page left* **Visiting the magnificent mosques of Tehran, Iran.** *right* **Walking in the most orthodox neighborhood in Jerusalem, Israel.**

קונים ומוכרים
טל. 050-2381121

# ENCHANTE GALLARDO
# THE FREEDIVER

*Being in the ocean, disconnected from everything else and present with Mother Nature, creates a sense of balance.*

My relationship with the water began when I was a young girl. Growing up in Hawai'i, I had always spent time in or around the water, but my love affair with the ocean really began when I started surfing. For me, surfing has been many things—I think the most important is a form of therapy. Floating there, in the water, you learn to sync to the movement of the ocean in order to be in the right spot to catch a wave. Being in the ocean, disconnected from everything else and present with Mother Nature, creates a sense of balance. I have to move in unison with her to enjoy a feeling that I wasn't able to find in any other aspect of my life at the time. Surfing taught me to respect the ocean in all of her moods. I am amazed by how calm and healing she can be, and then in a moment, she can shift to being dangerous and even fatal. Yet I always return to her.

In the ocean, I realize how small we are. Submerged in the water, suspended, feeling its embrace, I feel at home, like an embryo in the womb of Mother Earth. We are all a part of her, her children, and that is why the water can be so healing. Like a child looking to be consoled, we run to our mother for comfort.

Before I started freediving several years ago, I was in a transitional phase in my life and I felt lost. I had no idea what I wanted to do or what I was passionate about. I loved surfing but it was just a hobby. I had always wanted to travel while being engaged in something that I was passionate about. A saying that sticks in my mind and deeply resonates is, "Do what sets your soul on fire." When I discovered freediving, it was something I had an affinity for. I think surfing helped with that, because I already felt comfortable in the water. Ever since I started this freediving journey, it seems like everything has started to fall into place and given me a profound feeling that I was on the right path. It may have happened later in life, but I feel lucky to have found it.

Freediving deepened my connection with the ocean. Who would have known that the love I already had for her could only become more profound? Through the experience of descending into the depths, I am engulfed by peace. I feel one with this element, and often cannot discern the difference between my own body and the water. I try to meditate on land and am not able to reach the same level of presence as I do in the water. It is an experience that forces me to be present. It has allowed me to become more connected to both my body and—even more so—my mind. I am hyperaware of things that can evade my attention while on land, such as the slightest changes in the sensations of my body, and the thoughts that pop into my mind during a dive.

These connections led me to pursue freediving on a deeper level. I have also discovered fulfillment in the competitive aspect of freediving. I love to focus on training and competing on a world-class level. I find exhilaration in accomplishing the goals I have set in this arena. Competing pushes me to lead a healthier lifestyle, with a focus on diet, exercise, breath work, stretching, and yoga. I can be compulsive and find myself getting side-tracked easily. Training keeps me focused and motivated to be the best version of myself. It also provides many life lessons and personal growth. Although freediving allows me to challenge myself and my own personal limits, through these experiences

**In a shallow cenote in Tulum, Mexico. It is so nice to play around in the underwater garden here, simply enjoying and exploring the cenotes after the stress of competition.**

Sometimes, while enduring challenges, we feel isolated. But when we share these experiences with others, we come to the realization that we are not alone.

I can share the knowledge I have gained with others who are also on their own freediving journey.

One of the most fulfilling aspects of freediving for me is the camaraderie and the community. The bonds formed across the world show that no matter where you come from, we all share so much on a human level. Sometimes, while enduring challenges, we feel isolated. But when we share these experiences with others, we come to the realization that we are not alone. Support, encouragement, and care from others has fueled me through difficult times. I only hope I can do the same for others and inspire them to follow their dreams. Although we are on our own individual journeys through life, we are here supporting each other in unison. We share a passion that makes the struggles worthwhile. I am also thankful to have the support of my family, as without them I would not be able to pursue my freediving dreams.

Although I enjoy competing, there are many other aspects of freediving. I also love recreational diving, where I can swim through caves, 4-million-year-old lava tubes, or coral gardens, observing aquatic marine life. Sharing a space with marine life can be such a magical experience. It often feels like being suspended in a dream world. Interacting with these creatures brings a different perspective to my reality. When marine life chooses to interact with you, it is truly special. The

*left* **Looe Key is a coral reef that is located within the Florida Keys Marine Sanctuary, teaming with life from gigantic Goliath groupers, spotted eagle rays, reef sharks, turtles, and a variety of other species of fish. We lucked out this day with immaculate conditions: clear water and calm seas like a lake.**

*right* **Exploring the vibrant reef in Dahab, Egypt, fun diving with friends, and bringing out the camera to capture magical moments in the underwater world.**

Swimming through, my imagination runs wild and I feel like a wildlife adventurer, filled with the excitement of having to make it through in one breath.

exploration of caves all over the world and cenotes in the Yucatan is exhilarating. In this realm I feel my imagination run wild. Stalactites protrude from underwater ceilings. Rays of light penetrate and illuminate the water, shining like spotlights. It is like being on another planet, defying gravity, traveling through space and time.

When I first started working on boats, showing people the magic of the underwater world, I was just as fascinated. I learned to identify specific marine life by their behavior, looking for subtle cues such as patterns in the sand, or clumps of shells near holes in the reef. When I was able to spot something, I was overcome with rapture and curiosity, learning more each time.

I have always looked for caves and arches to swim through, especially when decorated with vibrant and lively corals. They mean the reef is healthy and abundant with life. If you pay attention to the little details, your attention can be taken by a small area, which encompasses a complex ecosystem. Sometimes you may find a reef shark or turtle tucked away as they rest in the shelter of the reef. At the entrances of caves, I often find schools of fish lingering beneath overhangs. Swimming through, my imagination runs wild and I feel like a wildlife adventurer, filled with the excitement of having to make it through in one breath. I enjoy the challenge. My senses are at their peak and I am elated just to be where I am. Nature is the best playground. The thought, "Can I just stay here forever?" permeates my mind. I wish that somehow I could breathe underwater.

Why do I freedive? I dive to discover the wonders of the world. The underwater world is a place of deep exploration and healing—internally and externally—and filled with a type of magic you can only find in the natural world. There is a sense of peace and calm. There, I feel eminently connected to the world and to myself. As a wanderer, I have always struggled with finding my place in the world. Society often tries to fit us into boxes. The water doesn't discriminate, it doesn't care who you are or where you came from, it accepts you. It embraces you in the good and bad. I can be whoever I want. I can float, swim, dive, yell out in excitement, cry, I can share special moments with other ocean dwellers such as whales, dolphins, turtles, sharks, whale sharks, or octopus. I am mesmerized by even the smallest of creatures, the various species of nudibranchs and Spanish dancers. It feels like weaving in and out of different dimensions of reality. When caught in the gaze of a whale, I feel my soul is captured. When swimming with whales or other large marine life, the perception of time seems altered. It seems as if the whales are doing a beautiful dance underwater in slow motion, then I look down at my legs and it seems that my fins are kicking much faster. In moments like these, it's easy to forget where I am. It's as if nothing else exists but that moment in time.

With the ocean I am free.
I am free to be me.
I throw tantrums,
I cry uncontrollably,
I laugh until my stomach hurts,
I sit suspended in silence,
Drifting with my thoughts.
There is a certain love I feel limited by my lexicon.
It's a feeling. A feeling of belonging,
A feeling of unconditional love,
Free to explore the world paired with the imagination.
A place to be without judgment or constructs.
A place to simply be.
I swim down to the bottom,
Enjoying the serenity and quiet.
I grab a handful of sand.
I feel the coarseness, the grains as they slip through my fingers.
I admire how everything, no matter how small or insignificant,
comes together to create this world of magic, of wonder.
I get to be a part of this.
I am a part of this magic.
I come to the realization. I too am magic.
I feel it wholly.

With all my ambitions, imperfections, and humanity, I too will soon become but a grain of sand. So, for as long as my body permits, I will venture out to seek the embrace of the ocean. Each experience with her is unique, like each individual that seeks these experiences. They never get old, and I never cease to be amazed.

Unbounded,
There is always more to discover.
It is a lifelong journey.
I feel like a child,
Eyes wide open.

Exploring the soul, body and mind.
In this realm I feel alive.

**An embryo in the womb of Mother Earth. Photo taken while exploring the beautiful reefs of Dahab, Egypt.**

# THE CONTRIBUTORS

## KRISTIN ADDIS
THE SOLO TRAVELER
bemytravelmuse.com
@bemytravelmuse

## BELÉN CASTELLÓ
THE BIKEPACKER
@belletoscan

## GINA JOHANSEN
THE EXPEDITIONIST
ginajohansen.com
@ginajohansen91

## AMANDA SPERAW
THE NOMADIC MAMA
@thisisbus

## ALIENOR LE GOUVELLO
THE HORSE TREKKER
@wild_at_heart_australia

## BETHSHEBA BLANKEN
THE SLOW TRAVELER
lostwithbeth.com
@lostwithbeth

## LIBBY DELANA
THE MORNING WALKER
libbydelana.com
@parkhere

## CAL MAJOR
THE SUP ADVENTURER
calmajor.com
@cal_major

## MANDY SHAM
THE NOMAD-ISH EXPLORER
orenji.club
@peach.punk

## MORGAN MATHERS
THE UNDERWATER EXPLORER
morganmathers.com
@fr0mthesea

## RACHEL ROSS
THE CANYONEER
rachelrossmedia.com
@rach4thesky

## ALICIA RIUS
THE URBAN EXPLORER
aliciariusphotography.com
@aliciariusphoto

## PAIGE VINCENT
THE STORM CHASER
paigevincent.darkroom.tech
@paigevincent

## SANDI OLUOCH
THE CURIOUS ADVENTURER
sandravertigo.com
@sandi.oluoch

## NESS KNIGHT
THE SURVIVALIST
nessknight.com
@ness_knight

## SHALEE WANDERS
THE ADVENTURE TRAVELER
shaleewanders.com
@shaleewanders

## LUCY SHEPHERD
THE EXPEDITION LEADER
lucy-shepherd.com
@lucysheps

## JILL HEINERTH
THE CAVE DIVER
intotheplanet.com
@jillheinerth

## CARME FONTANET
THE NEXT-LEVEL SOLO TRAVELER
@viajaralodesconocido

## ENCHANTE GALLARDO
THE FREEDIVER
@enchantedfreedive

# PHOTO CREDITS

## A

ALEX ST. JEAN
alexstjean.com
@alexstjeanphoto
*Page:* 227

ALICIA RIUS
aliciariusphotography.com
@aliciariusphoto
*Pages:* 142 - 145 - 146 - 147
149 - 150

AMANDA SPERAW
@thisisbus
*Pages:* 42 - 45 - 46 - 47 - 49
50 - 51 - 52 - 53

ARIZTON PAMPLONA
*Page:* 109b

## B

BETHSHEBA BLANKEN
lostwithbeth.com
@lostwithbeth
*Pages:* 71 - 72 - 73 - 74 - 76
77 - 78 - 79 - 80 - 81
82 - 83

BILL CHURCH
billchurchphoto.com
@billchurchphoto
*Pages:* 129 - 137

## C

CARME FONTANET
@viajaralodesconocido
*Pages:* 216 - 217 - 219t - 220
221 - 222 - 223 - 224
225

CAT VINTON
catvphotography.co.uk
@catvinton
*Pages:* 4 - 55 - 56 - 57 - 59
60 - 61 - 62 - 64 - 65
66 - 67 - 68

CODY MAYER
codymayer22.com
@codymayer22
*Pages:* 153 - 159

## D

DANIEL J.SCHWARZ
danieljschwarz.com
@danieljschwarz
*Page:* 233

DAVID MARCU
@marcu.david
*Page:* 236

## G

GARRETT FIDALGO
*Pages:* 11 - 15 - 17

GINA JOHANSEN
ginajohansen.com
@ginajohansen91
*Page:* 37

## I

IAN FINCH
ianefinch.com
@ianefinch
*Page:* 177

## J

JACKIE WINDH
jacquelinewindh.com
*Page:* 209

JAKE SMITH
jakesmithphoto.com
@jakesmithphoto
*Page:* 185

JAMES APPLETON
jamesappleton.co.uk
@jamesappletonphotography
*Pages:* 2 - 93 - 94 - 95 - 97 - 98
99 - 102 - 103

JANE KANG
*Pages:* 166 - 171l

JAVIER PARDINA
@pardina_studio
*Page:* 219br

JILL HEINERTH
intotheplanet.com
@jillheinerth
*Pages:* 207 - 211 - 213b

JOHN KOWIT
jkowitzphotography.com
@j.kowitz
*Page:* 228

JON WILLIAMS
jon-w.com
@jon_w
*Page:* 180b

JOSH SUPER
@jlsuper
*Pages:* 195 - 196

## K

KAYLEE MADDOX
@kayleethedreamer
*Pages:* 191tr - 193

b - bottom
t - top
r - right
l - left

12
13
14
15
16
Warwick
Burleigh Heads
Coolangatta
Tweed Heads
Murwillumbah
Pottsville
Brunswick Heads
Byron Bay
Lismore
Lennox Head
Ballina
Evans Head
Tenterfield
RANGE
Yamba
Grafton
DIVIDING
Arrawarra
Woolgoolga
Sandy Beach
Emerald Beach
Dorrigo
Coffs Harbour
Sawtell
Bellingen
Urunga
Armidale
OXLEY
WILD RIVERS
Macksville
Nambucca Heads

A member of Penguin Random House Verlagsgruppe GmbH
Neumarkter Strasse 28 · 81673 Munich


This edition published by agreement with Carolina Amell
www.amellcarolina.com



Cover: Photo by Shalee Wanders
Back cover: Photos by Cat Vinton (top left), Bethsheba Blanken (top right and bottom right), Peiman Zekavat (middle), Perrin James (bottom left)

Library of Congress Control Number is available; a CIP catalogue record for this book is available from the British Library.



Editorial direction: Julie Kiefer
Concept and coordination: Carolina Amell
Photo research: Carolina Amell
Design and layout: Carolina Amell
Copyediting: Martha Jay
Production management: Luisa Klose
Separations: Ludwig Media, Zell am See
Printing and binding: DZS Grafik d.o.o., Ljubljana

Penguin Random House Verlagsgruppe FSC® N001967

Printed in Slovenia

ISBN 978-3-7913-8920-2

www.prestel.com